Irreplaceable
A history of England in 100 places

Irreplaceable
A history of England in 100 places

Philip Wilkinson

Published by Historic England, The Engine House, Fire Fly Avenue, Swindon SN2 2EH
www.HistoricEngland.org.uk

Historic England is the public body that helps people care for, enjoy and celebrate England's spectacular
historic environment, from beaches to battlefields to parks and pie shops. We protect, champion and
save the places that define who we are and where we've come from as a nation. We care passionately
about the stories they tell, the ideas they represent and the people who live, work and play among them.

Since 1887 Ecclesiastical has been trusted to protect much of the UK's irreplaceable heritage and art.
A financial services company with a charitable purpose, we are the leading insurer of Grade I listed
buildings and are involved in insuring 10 of the UK's world heritage sites. We're a passionate supporter
of heritage skills, investing in projects that will help ensure the future of today's heritage.

First published 2018

ISBN 978-1-84802-509-7

British Library Cataloguing in Publication data
A CIP catalogue record for this book is available from the British Library.

The right of Philip Wilkinson to be identified as author of this work has been asserted by him in
accordance with the Copyright, Designs and Patents Act 1988.

For more information about images from the Archive, contact Archives Services Team,
Historic England, The Engine House, Fire Fly Avenue, Swindon SN2 2EH; telephone (01793) 414600.

Brought to publication by Sarah Enticknap and Paul Backhouse, Historic England.
Typeset in Adobe Caslon Pro 9/12pt
Page layout by Hybert Design Limited, UK
Printed in Belgium by Graphius

Front cover: Angel of the North, Gateshead
Frontispiece: Birkenhead Park, Wirral

Contents

Foreword

It is always possible to be in two times at once. Walking down a suburban, privet-proud street in the UK there are not only the obvious signs of Victorian, Edwardian and inter- and post-War brio, but flourishing fruit trees in the front gardens could reveal to the passer-by that this fertile earth was once tended by medieval monks as an apple orchard. Or, deep under the hedgerows of remote, rural land, the discovery of a Roman sword or a Byzantine coin is a clue that this modest spot was, in antiquity, at the centre of hyper-connected empires that stretched across continents. The hopes and tears and dreams and truths of other lives, and of other times can be found all around us if we just know where to look. From the majestic to the miniscule, we never simply live in the here and now; the past is constantly present. Which is why celebrating 100 historic places that matter to all of us – and that in their own way have shaped the story of the world – is such a brilliant, and brilliantly forward-looking, initiative.

As historians we've always argued that the past matters. The great news now is that neuroscientists are on our side. They tell us that we carry memory right across our brains – that all future thoughts are constructed from experiences or memories gone by. Simply put, we are creatures of memory. But all our memories are different – we remember the past, and care about it in unique and bespoke ways. There are as many truths about history as there are ways to be human. It is particularly appropriate then that the initial selection of these wonderful places was made by the general public, as part of the Irreplaceable campaign conducted by Historic England and supported by Ecclesiastical. Experts and champions Baroness Tanni Grey-Thompson, Monica Ali, David Olusoga, George Clarke, Mary Beard, Tristram Hunt, David Ison, Will Gompertz, Lord Robert Winston and myself then had the delightful task of choosing our particular stars. I know, without exception, we were all introduced to places and stories new to us, but which we'll now never forget.

There are some particularly resonant categories. We have all watched in horror as not just the lives, but the work and inspiration of the lives of man – temples, sculptures, engravings – have been destroyed in conflict zones across the world. So championing places that have suffered loss or destruction – from the Hillsborough Stadium to the ruins of Whitby Abbey in North Yorkshire, as Dame Mary Beard does, is a vital business. In the year that we celebrate 100 years since the 1918 increase in suffrage (for both women and men) it also felt appropriate to highlight this nation's proud history of protest. I'm always deeply touched by the fact that grassroots protests through time offered up change and opportunity for so many, from those campaigning for parliamentary reform in St Peter's Fields to those battling against fascism on Cable Street. And intellectual revolutions too – in arts, literature and science – the *Angel of the North* or the Minack Theatre, the work in Bletchley Park or the Jenner Hut in Gloucestershire – have all hugely enriched our shared experience. We live our lives thanks to the vision and commitment of many brave women and men from history.

So, if this book inspires you to visit one of the gardens chosen by George Clarke – from the magnificence of Windsor Castle to the modesty of the almshouses of the Hospital at St Cross, or to enjoy the sporting and leisure treasures loved by Tanni Grey-Thompson, such as the gentility of Lords Cricket Ground or the inspiration of Stoke Mandeville, or the locus of pioneering political movements championed by David Olusoga, the village of Tolpuddle or Bristol Bus Station, perhaps take a moment out to remember the debt we all owe to those who have gone before us.

Similarly, locations that have nourished faith and belief can be a balm for the mind of the living as they were for the long-dead. Whatever your beliefs (or none), the wonderful, thoughtful selection of places here, including the Holy Island of Lindisfarne and the Jewish Cemetery near Falmouth, could give us all the chance to take a moment out to recall that history reminds us to remember, to think better.

I was personally particularly inspired by the travel selection. Mankind loves to travel. Increasingly bone evidence tells us that historic populations were zigzagging across continents the whole time. Physiologically we're nomads, so charting where and how we've elected to travel through time is a fascinating experience.

So how to choose from the fabulously eclectic long list I was offered? Among my top 10 was a remnant from the dawn of the railway age in Darlington, an inn in Nottingham said to have been favoured by crusading knights, and a pier in Somerset once hailed by John Betjeman as the most beautiful in England. As an advocate of the ancient world I also couldn't resist the Fosse Way, one of Britain's longest and most important Roman roads and the Roman baths at Bath. Whenever on a family car journey – whether in my own childhood or as a parent – we would try to spot Roman roads, those confident structures which carve their way through the landscape, and sparked by this campaign I've spent many happy hours thinking of the Romano-British pilgrims who journeyed to Bath along lost Roman roads to the sanctuary of the goddess Sulis-Minerva.

Of course the Roman road was a double-edged sword. These engineering marvels expanded the country, allowing people to communicate, to mix and to share ideas, but they were also a way for the Romans to mark the land out as their own. 'We've arrived', these roads declared, 'forget us at your peril.' That said, archaeological remains close to the roads often share remarkable truths of the deep history of England. Recently, in Leicester, archaeologists excavated a Roman cemetery where several of the skeletons seem to be of African ancestry. One of our great strengths is that we're such a beautifully mixed-up, mongrel nation.

The fact that we love to explore beyond borders and boundaries says something very hopeful to me about humanity. As a species we're driven to connect, to reach out, to exchange goods and trade ideas and experiences. That's what these 100 places represent for me: they embody big ideas but they're also beautiful in and of themselves, forged through the wit, will and wisdom of the men and women of the past. And the places selected in both the Industry, Trade and Commerce and Art, Architecture and Sculpture categories, from the Blue Anchor Pub in Cornwall to Cromford Mills, Derbyshire, from the Brontë's parsonage to the Haçienda in Manchester, show how rich and diverse the human experience has long been on these islands.

'Plat', the root of the word place right the way back to Ancient Greece, and before that in the prehistoric mother tongue of Asia and Europe (Proto-Indo-European), meant a broad area or space – something that was spread. Celebrating and nourishing the historic places around us gives our minds space to think; engaging with these wonderful 100 places allows us to broaden minds a hundred times over – and to spread the love of our shared histories and stories across the ages.

Bettany Hughes

1 Science and Discovery

Bletchley Park
BUCKINGHAMSHIRE

Bletchley Park, a Victorian country house with a complex of 20th-century huts adjoining it, was the top-secret home of government code-breakers during World War II. At Bletchley Park, hundreds of people deciphered enemy military messages, analysed them, and passed them to the War Office, Admiralty, and Air Ministry. The code-breakers' work was outstandingly successful. They broke supposedly uncrackable German encryption systems such as Enigma, gathering information that had a major impact on key campaigns of the war such as those in North Africa and the D-Day landings; they helped restrict the damage caused by Luftwaffe bombers; and they enabled British naval commanders to track German U-boats and protect vital convoys bringing supplies from America. This work is said to have shortened the war by up to two years and saved many thousands of Allied lives.

Code-breaking was intensive work that required well-trained, logical minds. Many of the people at Bletchley were brilliant mathematicians; linguistic skills were also important. Much of the work was precise and methodical – but Bletchley Park also needed people who could think outside the box. To begin with, a small team occupied the house and its outbuildings. But the leaders of what was originally known as the Government Code and Cypher School became highly skilled in selecting the right people and found them in large numbers – especially after October 1941 when senior staff appealed directly to Churchill for more resources.

From that time on, buildings on the site mushroomed, as a series of brick, concrete and prefabricated huts were erected to house concentrations of code-breakers and 'traffic analysts'. These huts are preserved, together with many of their contents, giving a vital insight into Bletchley Park's contribution to World War II. However, the site was important not only for shortening the war. It was also home to the world's first electronic computer, Colossus.

Computers became important at Bletchley because of the sheer size of the code-breakers' task. Processing the huge amount of information coming in from the wireless intercept stations needed hundreds of people and took time. The job was particularly hard because the Enigma machines were so complex and were reset every day to produce a bewildering number of permutations. In order to decrypt messages, code-breakers had to know the settings used on that particular day. They were soon devising ways of speeding up the process mechanically.

At the beginning of the war Alan Turing, leader of Hut 8 at Bletchley Park, devised an electromechanical machine called the Bombe to help discover the daily settings of the Enigma machines used to encrypt incoming Axis messages. The Bombe was crucial to code-breaking work at Bletchley Park, but not all Axis messages were sent using Enigma. The Germans had a still more complex system, nicknamed 'Fish' by the British. To help break this, the British telecommunications engineer Tommy Flowers developed Colossus, a machine that stored information on paper tape and processed it with hundreds of glowing thermionic valves. Colossus was the world's first programmable, digital, electronic computer.

The Colossus machines were unknown to the general public and the scientific community after the war. Most were destroyed and two were kept secretly by Bletchley Park's successor organisation, GCHQ. The machines could not therefore have a direct influence on the post-war development of computing. However, the background knowledge gained by the people who worked at Bletchley Park fed into that later development, making Britain a leading player in the theory and design of computers. Turing's work, in particular, still informs thinking about computers and fields such as artificial intelligence. The mansion of Bletchley Park, together with the motley collection of buildings around it, has helped to shape our world.

Manning & Son, Printers, Greenwich. S. E.   GREENWICH, ROYAL OBSERVATORY   a 890|676

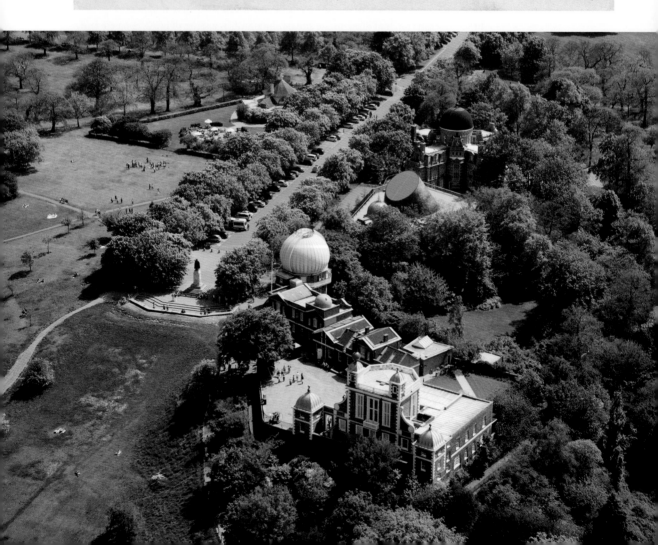

Royal Observatory Greenwich

LONDON

On 10 July 1676 John Flamsteed, the Astronomer Royal, moved into his new home, a combination of house and observatory, on the top of Greenwich Hill. The site had been selected by Sir Christopher Wren, who was the architect of the original building and himself a noted astronomer. Wren had chosen the site because its hill-top site gave excellent, uninterrupted views and because he could reuse the foundations of the old Greenwich Castle. What he did not know was how the observatory would grow, and how important the place would become in several related fields – geography, astronomy, and the measurement of time.

In the late 17th and early 18th centuries, one of the most pressing problems in navigation was how to calculate longitude. To work out their exact longitude in the open sea, sailors need to know the precise time at the place of departure (an hour of time difference equates to a 15 degrees difference in longitude). In the 17th century there were no clocks that would keep accurate time at sea, so this was impossible. Producing a suitable clock proved to be a long struggle, undertaken by the great 18th-century British clockmaker John Harrison. Because of the role of astronomers in Harrison's work, all four of his beautiful and elaborate timekeepers are on display at Greenwich.

By the early 19th century, Greenwich was seen as the home of timekeeping in Britain, and in 1833 the Astronomer Royal, John Pond, inaugurated the famous time ball, to provide a daily time signal for the general public. Every day, at 12.55 pm, the large red ball at the top of Wren's building (now known as Flamsteed House) rises to the top of its mast. At exactly 1 pm, it falls to the bottom again. Because of the observatory's hill-top site, the time ball can be seen from miles around, making the time check available to many, including those passing on the Thames.

Time is inscribed into the site at Greenwich in another way too. In 1884, Greenwich was selected by an international conference as the site of the prime meridian, the zero line of longitude from which all others are measured. The course of the line was marked in the ground by a brass (later stainless steel) strip, and since December 1999 by a laser beam that shines out of the observatory building northwards across the sky.

Flamsteed House was extended over the centuries and the site expanded to house new facilities and instruments as astronomy developed and as the Royal Observatory became more like a scientific institute than the base of a particularly prestigious homeworker. One of the most striking of these more recent structures is the dome housing the Great Equatorial Telescope, an instrument completed in 1893 to observe double star systems. This is a 28-inch refracting telescope (the largest refracting telescope in the UK) and its mount allows it to be turned on the same axis as the Earth, meaning that the observer can track a star as it moves across the sky.

The observations made with the Great Equatorial Telescope were particularly successful, and the instrument's distinctive onion dome has become as familiar a part of the view at Greenwich as Wren's Flamsteed House. The dome itself is a replacement – it was originally made of paper mâché, but after bomb damage during World War II a fibreglass dome was substituted. In spite of this change, the dome is just as much of its time as the Enlightenment-period architecture of Flamsteed House is of the 17th century, the whole site summing up in its appearance several centuries of groundbreaking science at Greenwich.

Today the Royal Observatory Greenwich is a museum, where visitors are amazed by the glistening mechanical beauty of Harrison's clocks and inspired by the ways in which Greenwich has changed history, transforming life at sea and opening up new fields of knowledge about the universe.

Jodrell Bank Observatory

MACCLESFIELD, CHESHIRE

The Jodrell Bank Observatory, part of the University of Manchester, has played a pioneering role in the history of radio astronomy. Its telescopes have enabled astronomers to do very important research on meteors, quasars, pulsars, masers, and other phenomena, and the site became world-famous for its work in tracking early space probes such as the Soviet Sputnik 1. Still fully functioning, Jodrell Bank is one of the most important observatories in the world.

The story of the radio telescope begins in 1945 when Bernard Lovell, an astronomer who had worked on radar during World War II, came to Manchester to study cosmic rays. He soon discovered that radio interference from the city's trams made observations impossible in the centre of Manchester, so he moved out to the university's botanical station at Jodrell Bank, some 20 miles from the city centre.

Research at Jodrell Bank, especially Lovell's work on meteors, went well, and by the early 1950s Lovell was planning a huge radio telescope, with a dish 250 feet in diameter. When completed in 1957, the Mark I Telescope was the largest steerable radio telescope in the world and the huge dish, now called the Lovell Telescope, still overlooks the site at Jodrell Bank. Today there are only two larger telescopes of this type. The Mark I was soon world famous. On 4 October 1957, the USSR launched its Sputnik 1 satellite. The astronomers at Jodrell Bank were able to track the Sputnik's booster rocket – the Mark I was the only telescope in the world that could achieve this, confirming to a sceptical public that the Russians' claim to have launched the earth-orbiting satellite was true. The telescope scored further successes tracking space probes, including – this time at the Soviets' request – tracking and receiving photographs from Luna 9, the Russians' unmanned moon lander.

The tracking of space probes won Jodrell Bank much publicity, but this was a small part of the observatory's work. Still more significant were its observations of pulsars and quasars, and the discovery of phenomena such as gravitational lenses and Einstein rings. The Lovell Telescope continues to operate, along with its companion Mark II elliptical telescope. The pair work not only independently but also as part of MERLIN, an array of seven telescopes spread across England.

Jodrell Bank today is a large site containing laboratories and a visitor centre as well as the large telescopes. However, it is still dominated by the enormous structure of the Lovell Telescope. The vast dish is held on two steel towers, each topped with a giant bearing that supports the dish and allows it to move. Some of the hardware, such as the gear racks that enable the dish to turn, came from the gun turrets of battleships HMS *Royal Sovereign* and HMS *Revenge*. The telescope was originally controlled by an electromechanical analogue computer (very old technology now, but very new in the 1950s), which drove two sets of motors, to move the dish around and simultaneously tilt it so that it could track an object moving across the heavens.

Since 2000 the Lovell Telescope has been thoroughly upgraded, with a new galvanised steel surface for the dish, replacement of part of the circular track on the ground that allows the instrument to turn, and an improved drive system. The 60-year-old telescope is thus still playing a role at the cutting edge of astronomical research. However, much of the original structure and design of the telescope remains – it is very much the instrument it was when Bernard Lovell conceived it in the 1950s. So for its importance in the history of science, its remarkable design and engineering, and its central position at Jodrell Bank, the Lovell Telescope, and the Mark II, are Grade I listed buildings, their great historical as well as their scientific importance given deserved recognition.

Ouse Washes

CAMBRIDGESHIRE

The Ouse Washes are a narrow strip of land stretching about 18.6 miles between Earith, near St Ives in Cambridgeshire and Downham Market in Norfolk, occupying an area of about 6,178 acres. The Washes are a Site of Special Scientific Interest. Often underwater in winter, they provide a major wintering area for a range of wildfowl and waders, and have a very rich flora. The Washes are Britain's largest washland (grazing land that is flooded in winter) and the area's importance as a wetland habitat is recognised internationally.

The Ouse Washes have a long history. They were created in the 17th century, when King Charles I granted a charter to Francis Russell, 4th Earl of Bedford, to drain lands on the fens of Cambridgeshire, opening up much of the marshy fenland for agriculture and promising great profits for those involved in the scheme. Work began in 1630 and by 1637 the Bedford River (now known as the Old Bedford River) had been cut to carry away flood water and provide a straighter channel to the sea than the existing River Great Ouse. This work has been credited to the Dutch engineer Cornelius Vermuyden, although it is uncertain whether he was actually involved in the scheme. Running in a straight north-easterly line, the original Bedford River was certainly a direct route, but it was not big enough to contain the flood waters or the high tides.

By the early 1650s, Cornelius Vermuyden had taken charge of the drainage system. He dug a second new channel, parallel to the first, called the Hundred Foot Drain and also known as the New Bedford River. This left a long, narrow strip of land between the two rivers. The rivers' inner banks were lower than their outer banks, and this meant that when the channels overflowed, the flood water flowed on to the strip of land between while the surrounding fens were left relatively dry. The water was held in the washland, gradually draining away to the sea. Vermuyden's scheme was completed in 1652. Farmers could use the washes for grazing in the summer; the land outside the washes was used for growing crops.

The creation of the Ouse Washes seemed to provide the solution for the drainage of the Fens. In fact, half a century later the fens were getting flooded again, because areas had dried out so much that they were lower than the rivers. In response, schemes were begun in the 18th and 19th centuries to dig ditches around field boundaries and build wind pumps to lift the water to the level of the rivers. The Ouse Washes continued to play a vital role in draining the Fens.

Today the Ouse Washes are known above all for their wildlife. Visitors come to the RSPB Ouse Washes Nature Reserve near Manea in the winter to see flocks of thousands of ducks (including garganey and widgeon) together with whooper and Bewick's swans; this is also a good time to see birds of prey, such as merlins, short-eared owls, hen harriers and peregrines. In springtime the reserve is home to many waders (such as avocet, snipe and redshank) which come to breed, as well as ducks such as shovelers and tufted ducks. The summer months are less good for seeing birds, because the grass is long, but the Washes are rich in butterflies, moths and dragonflies, and there are many colourful wild flowers. WWT Welney Wetland Centre, further down the Washes, plays host to a similar range of bird and plant life.

The Ouse Washes are a good example of the way in which human intervention has changed a landscape, and how this has had unintended benefits in creating a wildlife habitat that is also outstandingly beautiful. What was an impassable and impractical landscape before the 17th century has become an irreplaceable one in the 21st, to the advantage of farmers, visitors and wildlife alike.

Calder Hall Nuclear Power Station

SELLAFIELD, CUMBRIA

On 17 October 1956 Britain's nuclear age began when Queen Elizabeth II opened the nuclear power station at Calder Hall, Cumbria. Calder Hall was the world's first nuclear power plant to generate energy on a commercial scale. It was the first of a series of nuclear power stations built in the United Kingdom, and was at the time seen widely as a triumph of technology and engineering and as a symbol of hope for the future. Calder Hall promised to usher in an era of low-cost energy: eventually Britain's nuclear power stations produced 10 per cent of the electricity used in the United Kingdom.

A further three reactors were added to the station's initial one in the years after 1956, and further nuclear power stations followed in the 1960s. In one sense Calder Hall delivered on its promise. The power station was designed to run for 20 years before decommissioning. It did not close until 2003, meaning that the first reactor had been working for 47 years.

When it opened, Calder Hall was hailed as a marvel of engineering. Its four 88-metre high cooling towers became local landmarks, their characteristic hyperbolic design (the round towers tapering slightly to form concave curving sides) instantly recognisable. Next to them were four rather more anonymous square towers that contained the precision equipment that produced the nuclear reactions that powered turbines to produce electricity. The complex was developed before the era of computer-aided design, and its components were produced using the kind of machine tools developed to build military equipment during World War II. For the reactors to work, and work safely, the parts had to be produced to very fine tolerances, and the engineers were justly proud of their achievement. The power station proved successful and eventually became part of a large complex of buildings at Sellafield concerned with nuclear technology.

However, that technology has always been controversial. From the beginning, the generation of electricity at Calder Hall went in parallel with the production of fuel for nuclear weapons. The programme of the 1956 opening ceremony showed the importance of this part of the scheme: 'Calder Hall was built as a requirement for more military plutonium and as an experiment to investigate the possibilities of adapting nuclear energy to the production of electrical power quickly, cheaply and safely.' There was also the question of the safety of nuclear power. The accident at neighbouring Windscale in 1957, when a reactor caught fire, made it clear how critical the safety issue was. Finally, a key part of the case for nuclear power generation – its apparent cheapness – ignored the costs of waste disposal and decommissioning the power plant at the end of its life. In spite of these issues, Calder Hall and the power stations that followed it have a major historical importance, in that they hugely increased the amount of electricity available in the UK, and in the hope they offered for the benefits that would be brought by new technologies in the late 20th century.

In 2003 the process of closing and decommissioning Calder Hall began. It is due to finish in 2020 – currently the reactor buildings remain, surrounded by structures such as the famous spherical Windscale advanced gas-cooled reactor, the prototype for the second generation of reactors that succeeded the Magnox design. This power plant, shut down in 1983, is now part of a project demonstrating the safe decommissioning of nuclear reactors.

From orbital satellites to lasers, electron microscopes to electronic computers, there were huge hopes for new technologies in 1960s Britain. The development at Calder Hall heralded this hope, and became its symbol. Although the technology it pioneered was controversial, it was a key part of this story of change and discovery, and it will be remembered long after the decommissioning process comes to an end.

Brown Firth Research Laboratories

SHEFFIELD

Sometimes the location of a building is more important to its historical importance than its architecture. The Brown Firth laboratories of the early 20th century were in an unassuming brick building in Attercliffe, north-west of Sheffield's centre. For most of the city's history, metalworking, especially iron and steel working, has been the main industry, and the Brown Firth laboratories played a key role in the development of stainless steel.

Iron and steel (the latter an alloy of iron and carbon) are the most useful and versatile materials, used in everything from buildings to cutlery, but they have one major weakness: corrosion. One of the people who solved this problem was British metallurgist Harry Brearley. Brearley's work on steel took a vital turn in 1908, when two Sheffield companies came together to form the Brown Firth Research Laboratories. It was here that Brearley produced what is generally recognised to be the world's first rustless, or stainless, steel.

As with virtually every story to do with technology, Brearley could only have achieved what he did by building on the work of others. In the 1820s, a number of scientists, including the Englishmen Farraday and Stoddard and the Frenchman Pierre Berthier, had noticed that some alloys of steel and chromium were resistant to attack by certain acids. However, they never managed to produce a steel with a high enough chromium content to be truly stainless. Later in the 19th century, metallurgists had got closer to the heart of the problem. They discovered that to make an effective alloy with a high chromium content, the amount of carbon in the steel needs to be low. By 1872, Englishmen Woods and Clark patented an alloy with 30–35 per cent chromium and 2 per cent tungsten – resistant to water and acid, and good enough to be called stainless steel. But this was difficult to produce until in 1895 the German scientist Hans Goldschmidt invented a process for making carbon-free chromium.

It was Henry Brearley at Brown Firth who put all this work together when in 1912–13 an arms manufacturer whose gun barrels were eroding away too quickly asked for help. Could Brearley produce a metal that would be resistant to erosion? The metallurgist decided to try alloys of chromium and iron, and came up with a formula containing 12.8 per cent chromium and 0.24 per cent carbon. This is generally accepted as the first commercially produced corrosion-resistant steel. Brearley called it 'rustless steel'.

Brearley saw potential in the new alloy beyond the small-arms business. He thought it would be widely applicable in Sheffield's cutlery industry and, when his own employers at Brown Firth were not enthusiastic, approached one of his school friends, Ernest Stuart, who was Cutlery Manager at Mosley's Portland Works. After a few weeks, Stuart had come up with a process that hardened the steel to make it suitable for knives, and the production of stainless steel cutlery began. Stuart was also the one who came up with name 'stainless steel'.

Stainless steel is now used in thousands of different applications all over the world. The material first made at Brown Firth is used in car and aeroplane engines, beer kegs and safety razors, office machines and exhaust pipes. It is found all over the homes of the developed world, in everything from door handles to saucepans. It is also widely used in buildings, both in high-tech structures such as the Calder Hall power station (*see* pp 10–11), but also in restoration projects in sensitive buildings where corrosion-resistant support is required; the structures of both St Paul's Cathedral and York Minster now benefit from stainless steel elements. The work done in the modest-looking building of the Brown Firth Laboratories truly changed the world.

Edward Jenner's House and Hut

BERKELEY, GLOUCESTERSHIRE

This 18th-century house in Berkeley, Gloucestershire, and the small hut in its garden were where some of the most important pioneering work in vaccination took place, leading ultimately to the eradication of the fatal disease smallpox and the saving of millions of lives. The house was the home of Dr Edward Jenner, who was born in Berkeley in 1749 and trained in surgery in Gloucestershire before going to London to work under the surgeon John Hunter at St George's Hospital. Jenner spent three years in London before returning to his home town to practise as a family doctor and surgeon. By 1785 he had bought himself the house in Berkeley, where he lived and worked.

Like every 18th-century physician, Jenner saw many patients die of smallpox. He also knew about the practice of variolation – infecting a patient with smallpox in the hope that they would get a mild form of the disease and develop immunity – through the work of Lady Mary Wortley Montagu. Lady Mary was wife of the British ambassador to Turkey, and brought the idea home with her, popularising variolation during the smallpox epidemic of 1721. Variolation often worked, but it was very risky because sometimes the patient caught the full-blown version of the disease and died.

Physicians such as Jenner took a different approach. They noticed that people who caught the milder disease cowpox became immune to smallpox. Cowpox is a similar disease to smallpox but is milder and can be transferred from animals to humans; physicians noticed that dairy maids often caught cowpox and rarely died of smallpox. Some people had even tried deliberately infecting patients with cowpox in the hope that they would become immune, but this procedure had not been tested scientifically. So Jenner applied scientific method to this knowledge and carried out some experiments in his surgery at Berkeley. In 1796 he inoculated an eight-year-old boy, James Phipps, the son of his gardener, by taking infected pus from a milkmaid who had cowpox and applying it to scratches on the boy's arm. The boy developed a fever, but recovered. Jenner then took the great risk of infecting him with material infected with smallpox; the boy did not develop the disease.

Jenner tested his result by performing the same procedure on some 23 other patients, none of whom caught smallpox; he presented his findings to the Royal Society and finally published his results. Not everyone accepted Jenner's findings immediately. But eventually the evidence was accepted, in part at least because Jenner had backed up his theories with proper scientific testing. He had shown that there was a safe way of preventing the deadly disease. The new procedure was called vaccination, from the Latin *vacca*, a cow, and *Variolae vaccinae*, Jenner's term for cowpox. By 1840, the much more dangerous practice of inoculation with smallpox had been banned and large numbers of people had been vaccinated.

Jenner himself found it easy to encourage his own patients in Gloucestershire to be vaccinated. The procedure was cheap, and country people were reassured because vaccination was based on an idea that was familiar to them – dairymaids did not get smallpox. He had a small hut built in his garden, which he used as a consulting room for his local patients. The hut was designed by Jenner's friend local clergyman Robert Ferryman. It is a rustic building, in a style fashionable at the end of the 18th century, with thatched roof and tree trunks on either side of the door, which itself has rustic wooden decoration. Jenner called it his Temple of Vaccinia, and local people queued there when they heard that Jenner's vaccinations were successful. It still stands as a shrine for those who wish to pay tribute to the doctor and scientist whose work ultimately led to the eradication of smallpox.

ICI General Chemicals Research Laboratory

WIDNES, CHESHIRE

Chemistry is a hugely important field, but, as with many sciences, it can be difficult to track down the exact place where discoveries happened. Laboratories are sometimes small buildings, often part of larger complexes such as universities or manufacturing companies, and as this is a rapidly changing field, buildings get demolished or repurposed. An example of this is the ICI General Chemicals Research Laboratory at Widnes, which was demolished to make way for roads serving the new Mersey Crossing bridge. However, its location remains important, because it was here that a chemist developed a compound that changed millions of lives.

The chemist was Charles Suckling (pictured below), and he first synthesised halothane in 1951. Halothane is one of the most important drugs ever produced – Professor Sir Robert Winston has described its significance as comparable to that of penicillin. Halothane is important because it is a safe and reliable inhaled anaesthetic.

Before the 1950s, physicians already had a range of anaesthetics at their disposal – both intravenous compounds and those that could be inhaled, such as ether and chloroform, which had been in use since the 1840s. However, ether and chloroform are dangerous substances. Ether is highly flammable, and the problems this posed increased as more and more electronic equipment was used in operating theatres. Chloroform is toxic to the liver. Halothane, by contrast, is much safer than previous anaesthetics and enabled patients to be given a general anaesthetic for an operation. It is less flammable than ether, it smells more pleasant, and is low in toxicity. It also works quickly, and has a pain-relieving effect after surgery.

Charles Suckling had been an ICI research chemist since 1942. During World War II he had worked with a group of chemicals called halogenated alkanes, which, among other things, were used in high-octane aviation fuel. Among these chemicals, he was particularly interested in the ones containing fluorine. It was by synthesising a range of these compounds that led Suckling to halothane, which he tested for its anaesthetic properties. Having synthesised the compound, Suckling embarked on a series of tests, culminating in a set of clinical trials supervised by Michael Johnstone, a Manchester anaesthetist. Suckling's systematic tests and trials are now recognised widely as among the first instances of designing a drug in the modern way.

Because we do not yet fully understand the way the brain's chemistry functions, it is not certain exactly how halothane (or other anaesthetics) work, but halothane has given comfort and pain relief to millions of patients, and stayed in regular use well into the 1980s. The compound revolutionised the field and led to a new era in anaesthesia, because it was the forerunner of a whole generation of other anaesthetics that are fast-acting, as well as causing less nausea and lacking the flammability of ether.

Suckling's laboratory no longer exists. The company for which he worked, which was a household name and produced a range of products, such as pharmaceuticals, paints, dyes, artificial fibres, explosives and polymers, disappeared in a takeover in 2008. The site of Suckling's discovery cannot be visited. However, the wall of the Catalyst Science Discovery Centre, further along the Waterloo Road from the site of the lab, bears a blue plaque remembering the synthesis and commercial development of halothane, making this location a 'National Chemical Landmark' and helping to ensure that the work of Suckling and his colleagues is remembered.

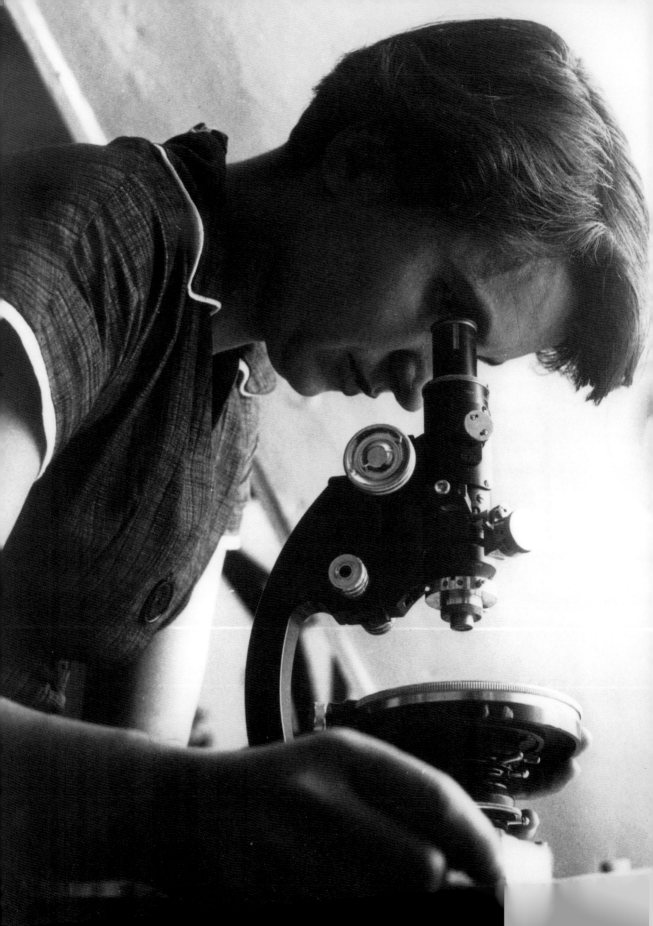

Medical Research Council Biophysics Unit

KING'S COLLEGE, LONDON

The year is 1952 and the setting is another of science's 'hidden' locations: a laboratory buried three floors below central London, part of the Strand campus of King's College. Among those working at King's were Maurice Wilkins and Rosalind Franklin, and Franklin's PhD student Raymond Gosling. Franklin's work as a chemist and X-ray crystallographer – especially her research on coal and, later, on the structure of viruses – made her well known in her field. But she and her colleagues also played a vital part in one of 20th-century science's most important discoveries: the structure of DNA.

By the 1950s, scientists had grasped that the DNA molecule was the substance that carried information about heredity from one organism to another. They knew the chemical formula of DNA, but they did not understand its structure, and therefore did not know exactly how it worked. Several scientific teams – in Cambridge, London and California – were working on the subject.

In May 1952 Gosling, working under Franklin's supervision, took an X-ray diffraction image of a sample of DNA. This kind of imaging works by exposing an object to X-rays; the X-rays bounce off the object in different directions, and this shows the scientist the internal structure of the object. Franklin (pictured) and Gosling applied this technique to a tiny piece of DNA, exposing it to X-rays for some 60 hours. When the X-rays scattered, they produced the small image now known as Photo 51, showing a cross shape on a white background. This result looked unassuming but Franklin and her colleague Maurice Wilkins knew it was significant. Without Franklin's knowledge, Wilkins showed it to Cambridge scientists James Watson and Francis Crick, who were researching DNA. For Watson and Crick it was the missing piece of a jigsaw puzzle, the evidence that, combined with their own work, allowed them to discern the double-helix structure of the DNA molecule.

The work of Watson, Crick, Wilkins, and Franklin opened up an entire field of science. In 1962 the first three of them received the Nobel prize for their work, but Franklin died in 1958 aged only 37 and the Nobel committee do not award posthumous prizes. Partly because of this, because of the fact that the enormous significance of DNA was not yet fully grasped, and also because of the attitude of some of her male colleagues, she did not originally receive the recognition she deserved for her work on DNA, although her research on coal and viruses was acclaimed in obituaries when she died. But today her place in the history of science is assured and Photo 51 has been called the most important photograph ever taken.

Franklin's subterranean laboratory was always out of the limelight but it has now vanished completely. The biophysics unit at King's was only five years old when Gosling and Franklin made their discovery, but it did not remain on the Strand site for long. It moved away in the 1960s, and is now based at the university's Waterloo campus, where it occupies part of the aptly named Franklin-Wilkins building.

Water pump, Broadwick Street
SOHO, LONDON

It is the most modest of monuments: a pavement water pump without a handle. But it held the secret of one of the most deadly diseases of the 19th century – cholera. The man who unlocked the mystery of the disease was a physician at London's Westminster Hospital called John Snow. He had a particular interest in infectious diseases and in 1850 was a founder member of the Epidemiological Society of London, which had been started after an outbreak of cholera in 1849. At this time the germ theory of disease had not been put forward and most physicians believed that infections were carried by what they called miasma, an invisible vapour made up of fragments of foul-smelling decaying matter. 'Foul air' containing miasma was thought to be the source of many diseases, and people found this easy to believe because in poor city areas insanitary, badly ventilated, crowded housing often harboured disease.

One of the most deadly diseases of the 19th century was cholera. Internationally, the death toll was enormous – in Tokyo alone between 100,000 and 200,000 people were killed by cholera in 1858–60. Although the figures in Great Britain were not quite so vast, the disease was still devastating. In 1848 some 52,000 people in Britain died in a major outbreak. In 1849 it took 14,000 lives in London alone. A further 10,000 lives were lost in the 1854 epidemic in London. Other British cities also had high death tolls.

John Snow was sceptical that miasma caused these deaths. When cholera broke out in Soho, London, in 1854, he and Henry Whitehead, assistant curate of St Luke's church, Soho, talked to the locals. One thing they discovered was that the victims got their water from one source: a pump in Broad Street (now Broadwick Street), at the corner with Poland Street. Nearly all the infected families lived near the pump. The few who lived nearer to another pump told Snow that they actually used the Broad Street pump because they preferred its water to that from their local pump, or their children attended a school near Broad Street. Snow was convinced that the water from Broad Street was causing the disease. He went to see the local council, and persuaded them to make the pump inactive by removing the handle. When they did this, new cholera cases declined and the epidemic died out.

It was clear to Snow that the epidemic was already in decline when they removed the pump handle. Many people moved away from the district – to escape the 'foul air'. But he was convinced of the link between cholera and infected water, and continued to study the problem. He plotted cholera cases on a map, and researched the way the water company supplied their water. He found that the company drew drinking water from a stretch of the River Thames that was polluted with sewage. A former cesspit was also polluting the water. He had found the root of the problem.

In spite of Snow's work, many people refused to believe his theory of how cholera was transmitted. It seems that the idea that people were in effect drinking sewage was simply too horrific for them to countenance. However, by 1866, people accepted that water was the problem: during a cholera outbreak at Bromley-by-Bow in the East End, people were told to boil all their drinking water. By the 1880s, thanks to the work of scientists such as Louis Pasteur in France and Robert Koch in Germany, germ theory at last became accepted and the memory of John Snow – who had died after a stroke in 1858 – was honoured. A water pump with its handle removed remains at the corner of Broadwick Street and Poland Street to mark his achievement, and, ironically, for Snow was a teetotaller, a pub on the street corner bears his name.

2 Travel and Tourism

Dreamland

MARGATE, KENT

Today there are amusement parks all over the world, and they continuously reinvent themselves to offer visitors the latest and most thrilling rides. Such attractions have a long history, none more so than Dreamland in Margate, the oldest surviving amusement park in Britain. Here visitors can enjoy a range of attractions from the big wheel and gallopers to the 'Scenic Railway', the country's oldest roller coaster.

Dreamland's story began in the 19th century, when visitors started to flock to the seaside on the newly built railways. In 1870 George Sanger, a charismatic circus proprietor, bought the dance hall and restaurant, the Hall by the Sea, on the site. He added a pleasure garden, sideshows and rides, but he died in 1911 and the attraction fell on hard times during World War I. In 1919, it was bought up by entrepreneur John Henry Iles, revamped, and renamed Dreamland.

Iles owned amusement parks all over Britain, and set up others around the world, from South America to Egypt. His travels took him to North America, where he visited the parks in Chicago and Coney Island, New York and was especially impressed with American roller coasters. He did a deal with the LaMarcus A. Thompson Scenic Railway Company to build, sell, and operate their Scenic Railway roller coasters in Europe. These were the most impressive rides of their time, in which small trains ran up and down slopes, reaching terrifying speeds.

When he redeveloped Dreamland, Iles invested £500,000 (roughly equivalent to £15M today) in the project and at its heart was a Scenic Railway roller coaster. It was an instant attraction – because few British people had ever experienced anything like it and its large curving wooden structure (roughly a mile in length) was visible from all over the town. Around the roller coaster Iles arranged other rides, quickly followed by a skating rink, and by 1923 there was also a cinema. This first cinema was followed in 1935 by the sleek Art Deco Dreamland Cinema, an ultra-modern 2,200-seater in the latest architectural style.

Dreamland was instantly popular. Some 500,000 people rode the roller coaster in the first three months of operation in 1920 and it remained a magnet for visitors through the 1930s. During World War II, Dreamland was requisitioned by the government to house troops, but some of these were members of ENSA and put on stage shows to add to the films screened in the cinema. The 1950s and 1960s saw it become one of the biggest music venues outside London, hosting bands like the Rolling Stones and The Who. Continuous adaptation, from bigger rides to more family-friendly attractions, ensured Dreamland's survival, but a decline set in at the end of the 20th century, resulting in the park's closure, and a devastating fire.

But Dreamland has risen from the ashes. A preservation campaign, major investment, and the restoration of the Scenic Railway, has brought the place to life once more. The park now showcases a collection of historic rides, with the Scenic Railway as its centrepiece. A host of modern attractions, from live entertainment to street food, bars to art installations, completes the mix. The setting near the beach combines scenery and convenience.

Britain has numerous theme parks, some with the latest in high-tech rides designed to give visitors the biggest thrills, some designed to appeal to younger families. But many of the older, smaller parks have closed, unable to compete with the spectacular rides provided by the major theme parks. None of the survivors has the heritage of Dreamland, which preserves historic rides from its early days along with buildings like the cinema that show its evolving history. Not only Britain's oldest theme park, it is also a living and working history of how these attractions have changed and developed and a vital part of the story of the British seaside.

Clevedon Pier

SOMERSET

Sir John Betjeman called it 'the most beautiful pier in England' and the 1,024-foot-long Clevedon pier is certainly elegant, its unusual structure providing supports that are at once strong, slender and curvaceous. Today it is a thriving tourist attraction, lovingly restored and home to a café and an art gallery. However, its origins go back to much more practical, utilitarian needs, and are rooted in the commercial realities of Victorian England.

With the coming of the railways a comprehensive transport network was created across Britain, linking London with almost every part of the country. One major obstacle in this network was the River Severn, which prevented a direct link between the capital and South Wales – trains between London and Cardiff had to take a long detour via Swindon and Gloucester. In 1847, however, the railway came to the quiet Somerset town of Clevedon, on the Severn Estuary, making a steamer link to South Wales possible.

The idea of building a pier for steamers to moor at Clevedon went back to the 1830s, before the railway arrived. Building work began, but high winds destroyed the structure before it was finished and the scheme was only revived in the 1860s. This time there were two engineers, John William Grover and Richard Ward, and they came up with an innovative idea for the pier's construction. They recycled a cache of rails that had been discarded from the broad-gauge South Wales Railway, designed by I K Brunel, to make the pier's main supports. These were so-called 'Barlow rails', named after their inventor W H Barlow and designed with a tapering profile so that they could be laid directly on to ballast, without sleepers. Laying track in this way caused maintenance problems, so the Barlow rails were replaced with standard rails. Unsuccessful for railway use, they proved ideal pier supports.

The building work was dangerous – the Severn has the second highest tidal range in the world. One worker lost his life and several others had to be rescued from drowning. But the work progressed swiftly, starting in July 1867 and reaching completion in February 1869. After a gala opening, the pier began offering a busy steamer service between Clevedon and South Wales with users taking advantage of the quicker journey. The pier's future seemed assured.

Everything changed in 1886, when the Severn Railway Tunnel opened, allowing trains to travel to South Wales directly. However, plans to improve the pier continued, with a new landing stage and enhanced pier head, on which a Japanese-style pagoda and a pair of shelters were erected; a dance hall was added in the early 20th century. Boats continued to call at the pier, and it also became a popular place for promenading and fishing. In the 20th century, the traffic was increasingly dominated by pleasure boats, with round trips taking in Weston-super-Mare and Ilfracombe, and shorter excursions to Bristol.

Although there was a decline in use, Clevedon pier survived until 1970, when two spans collapsed during a routine load test that was being carried out for insurance purposes. The pier head was left stranded, with a large gap between it and the intact part of the structure, and an uncertain period began before a restoration took place. After a painstaking project in which the structure was surveyed, reusable parts salvaged, and new components cast, the pier triumphantly reopened in 1998. New visitor facilities were added later and the pier is now well used by both locals and visitors. Two historic steamers, the *Balmoral* and the *Waverley*, still use the pier.

The history of Clevedon's pier follows a trajectory that is typical of many of England's seaside piers – from practical landing stage to leisure attraction, with a decline in the mid- to late-20th century as Britons began to holiday abroad in increasing numbers, leaving the old seaside resorts behind. Clevedon, however, shows that piers can have a bright future.

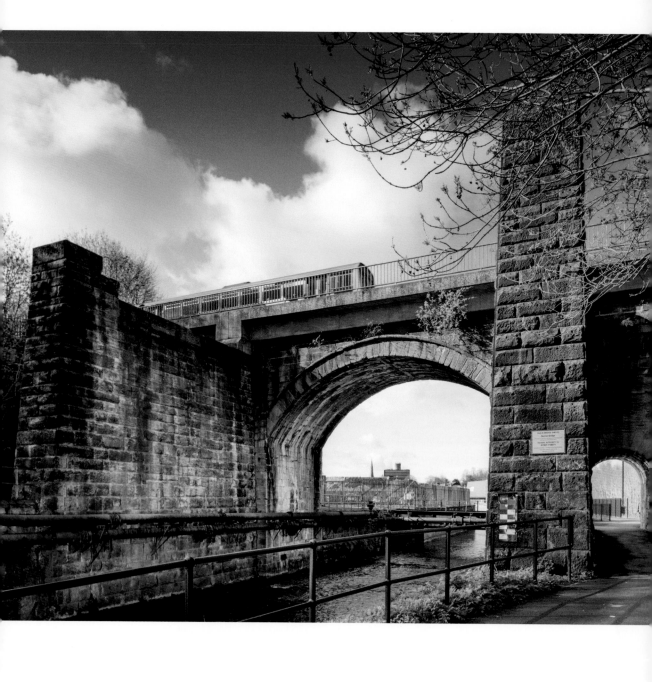

Skerne Railway Bridge

DARLINGTON, COUNTY DURHAM

The Skerne Bridge is the oldest railway bridge in continuous use in the world. Its solid stone structure has stood in the centre of Darlington since 1825, when the first steam-hauled, passenger-carrying railway opened between Stockton and Darlington, and it is an enduring symbol of the way the railways transformed Britain and much of the world. The railways made the rapid transport of goods and people a reality for the first time. They ran into the heart of towns and cities and connected sources of raw materials, manufacturing centres, and markets in a country-wide network, hugely stimulating industry and trade.

The basic elements of the railway already existed in 1825: some mines used horse-drawn wagons to transport coal or ore; steam engines were powering machinery in factories. The Stockton and Darlington Railway put these ingredients together and combined them with the engineering skills required to lay track, design locomotives and build bridges. The engineer behind the railway was George Stephenson, and he had to provide several bridges on the 26-mile route, including an innovative iron-truss bridge over the River Gaunless at West Aukland. The most enduring of these pioneering structures is the Skerne Bridge in Darlington itself.

For this important town-centre bridge Stephenson had the services of an architect, Ignatius Bonomi, who was Surveyor of Bridges for County Durham. Bonomi, an Englishman with Italian ancestors, worked widely in northern England, especially in County Durham. His office did jobs for Durham Cathedral and Durham Castle, but he is remembered today as the first railway architect. His very simple three-arch design is unremarkable visually – its main characteristic is solidity, and its strength served the railway and its successors well. Together with Stephenson's locomotives, it became one of the most familiar symbols of the railways, and featured on the Bank of England £5 note that was used between 1990 and 2003.

The Stockton and Darlington Railway was founded to serve the coal industry. It linked several coal mines to Stockton, where coal could be loaded on to steamers and sent to ports along the east coast. But passengers were carried from the beginning and people were impressed, even if at first the services were not regular and most of the early passenger trains were pulled by a horse.

In a few years, however, regular steam-hauled passenger trains were a reality and a revolution in travel and transport had begun. By the 1840s, railways were being built connecting major cities to London and long-distance rail travel was possible. By the late 19th century, fares were low enough to allow mass transport, making it possible for people to travel long distances to find work or even to take holidays. This revolution began when Stephenson and Bonomi built the Skerne Bridge in 1825.

Grand Hotel

SCARBOROUGH, NORTH YORKSHIRE

The British seaside holiday, so popular in the 20th century, first took off on a large scale not in one of the famous working-class resorts like Blackpool or Skegness, but in genteel Scarborough on the North Yorkshire coast. Here the enormous Victorian Grand Hotel still towers above the beach, a reminder of the town's long history as a resort.

Scarborough has a medieval castle, around which a market town and port developed, but in the 1620s there was a major change in the town's fortunes. A stream of acidic water, said to have health-giving properties, was discovered and Scarborough became a spa. By the 18th century, it was a flourishing resort, with people coming not only for the acidic water but also to enjoy sea bathing.

In 1845, the steady stream of visitors became a flood with the coming of the railways. That was the year in which Scarborough was linked to York by rail, and York was well connected, on one of the main north–south arteries, with links to Manchester, Nottingham, London, and beyond. Scarborough boomed, especially as the Crown, the town's first purpose-built hotel, was open for business when the railway opened.

Twenty years later, tourism to Scarborough was still growing and there was the need for yet more hotel accommodation. The Hull architect Cuthbert Brodrick, mainly famous as the designer of the enormous Leeds Town Hall and other Leeds buildings, came up with the solution: the Grand Hotel, one of the largest in the whole of Europe. When it opened, the Grand had 365 rooms and 52 chimneys, symbolising the number of days and weeks in a year. To complete the calendar symbolism, it also has 12 storeys if one counts the vast multistorey basement, itself larger than many sizeable hotels.

The Grand Hotel is vast and its site is designed to set it off to advantage. The building looms above the beach, dominated by its imposing four main floors, while the two-storey attic above and the tapering domes at each corner give it a distinctive silhouette. The material – yellow brick with terracotta dressings – makes it stand out still more. The architectural effect, with the corner domes and tall attic, is French, and very large, and this monster building was not only capacious but also a very good advertisement for itself and for the town. The hotel became famous, both for its size and for its facilities, like the double set of taps fitted to its baths, so that guests could bathe in either fresh or salt water. It drew more visitors to the town, ushering in Scarborough's Victorian heyday.

In the second half of the 19th century, many seaside hotels were built in Britain, as holidays by the sea became increasingly popular. The Grand Hotel therefore marks a turning point in the history of hotels. Before the railway age, few buildings bore the name 'hotel' at all. Towns had inns, where people travelling on horseback and by coach could put up for the night, breaking long journeys and changing horses before moving on the next day. Hotels as places where people stayed for an extended period were still relatively new, but buildings like Scarborough's Grand showed how impressive and attractive they could be.

Hotels like the Grand were aimed mostly at middle-class visitors, but members of the working class went to the seaside too – although they went mainly on day trips, which were also made possible by the railway network. With its vast size, bravura architecture, and prominent seaside site, the Grand is one of the great Victorian hotels. It stands as a lasting reminder of the popularity of the British coast and of a time when a holiday at the seaside was the annual highlight of many Britons' lives.

Helvellyn

CUMBRIA

For more than 200 years, people have been coming to Helvellyn, one of the most striking and evocative mountains in the Lake District. It scenic features, such as the spectacular ridges Striding Edge and Swirral Edge, and the small, lonely lake called Red Tarn, are unrivalled, and the views from the 3,117-foot summit extend for miles, taking in distant mountains and lakes such as Ullswater. Helvellyn is at the heart of one of England's most celebrated regions.

Although we think of the Lake District as a place of outstanding natural beauty, this was not always the case. In 1724 Daniel Defoe described it in his *Tour Through the Whole Island of Great Britain* as 'the wildest, most barren and frightful of any [place] that I have passed over in England'. This was the normal reaction of the time: people regarded mountainous scenery as barbarous and dangerously wild. They preferred gentler lowland landscapes that had been tamed by the 'civilizing' hand of humanity. By the later 18th century, however, this was beginning to change. Writers and artists were starting to appreciate wilder scenery and in 1778 the antiquary and priest Thomas West published *A Guide to the Lakes*, encouraging visitors to seek out viewpoints and admire the scenery. West's guide proved popular, but still more successful was the 1810 *Guide to the Lakes* by the poet William Wordsworth.

Wordsworth was one of the earliest appreciative visitors to Helvellyn, the Lake District's third highest peak, a few miles north of his home in Grasmere. The mountain is mentioned in Wordsworth's poetry too: he praises the grandeur and vast scale of the scenery, its waterfalls, its gulfs and abysses, and the striking effect of the light, and describes a climber's reaction as 'Awed, delighted, and amazed'. Poets like Wordsworth and his friend Samuel Taylor Coleridge helped people appreciate the beauty of the Lake District, and Helvellyn in particular. Although not the area's highest mountain, it was more accessible than its neighbours Scafell Pike and Sca Fell, and just as spectacular scenically.

One thing that early visitors such as Wordsworth liked about the Lake District was its loneliness. Here it was possible to get closer to nature because there were not many people around to spoil the view or the atmosphere. As Britain became more and more industrial, its cities crowded, noisy and polluted, places like Helvellyn were valued more and more. They were valued too because they were British: when they discovered the Lake District, British people realised that they did not have to go to the Alps to appreciate mountain scenery – in peaks like Helvellyn Britain had something that was as good as anything in Europe.

By the 1840s, the area was popular enough for the railway companies to see an opportunity. In 1844 there was a proposal to bring the railway to the Lake District. Wordsworth objected strongly. He feared that the area would be swamped with visitors, few of whom would truly appreciate the qualities of the landscape. True appreciation and understanding of romantic scenery, he thought, were not possible to uneducated people; he ended a letter objecting to the railway plans with the plea, 'Let then the beauty be undisfigured and the retirement unviolated'.

In spite of the objections, the railway came to the Lake District: to Kendal in 1846, to Windermere in 1847, and to further centres in the 1860s. This increased tourism to the Lakes hugely, allowing more people to appreciate the area than Wordsworth believed possible. In spite of the railways, however, and the later influx of tourists arriving by road, the Lake District remains outstandingly beautiful. Careful stewardship by landowners, especially the National Trust, and the creation of the Lake District National Park in 1951 have helped preserve its special qualities. In addition, the challenging gradients of many fells keep all but the most determined walkers away. Places like Helvellyn, therefore, have kept their character: quiet, windswept and grand.

The Fosse Way

One of the best known achievements of the Romans in Britain was their countrywide network of straight, well-made roads. The Fosse Way is one of the most important of them. It originally extended 230 miles from Exeter north-east to Lincoln via Bath, and between Ilchester in Somerset and Lincoln it runs 182 miles without deviating more than 6 miles from a straight line. Modern roads still follow much of the route – the A46 between Lincoln and Leicester, the B4455 in Warwickshire, and the A429 in Gloucestershire all make use of the route surveyed by the Romans almost 2,000 years ago. Other sections of the old road, particularly between Bath and Cirencester, are now tracks and byways, or are marked by hedges or boundaries, but for long stretches the Fosse Way is still a working highway.

The Fosse Way's original purpose was military: it was built by the Roman army in the early years of their occupation of Britain after AD43. The route connected a series of camps, including the two termini and Ilchester, Cirencester and Leicester. The camps were originally set up to defend the Romans' frontier with the local British tribes, but later grew into bigger civilian settlements – Cirencester became one of the largest towns in Roman Britain. The road, therefore, became an artery for administrators and traders as well as a military route. Most of the towns on the route were at junctions or crossroads, so as it made its long path across southern England and the Midlands, the Fosse joined Akeman Street and Ermin Way at Cirencester, Watling Street just south of Leicester, and Ermine Street at Lincoln.

Oddly, we do not know how the Romans themselves named their British roads. Roman roads on the European mainland were usually named after emperors. Britain's Roman roads have names given to them by the local population, probably in the post-Roman period.

Ermine Street, for example, takes its name from a tribe called the Earningas, who lived in parts of Cambridgeshire and Hertfordshire. The name of the Fosse Way comes from the Latin *fossa*, a ditch – either because of the drainage ditch that ran on either side of the road surface, a typical feature of Roman highways, or from the defensive ditch that was dug to mark and defend the western frontier of the Roman territory. It is a name that has endured. It is widely used on road signs and many people refer to driving along the Fosse Way even if they do not recall the 'official' number of the road.

Modern motorists on the A46 or A303 have reason to be grateful to the painstaking work of the Roman engineers who built the Fosse Way. Its straight course is clear to today's drivers along most stretches, and from aerial photographs that show its path through the green fields of the Midlands. The Roman road surface is long gone but the direct route and the connections to a wider road network remain. This network shows how the legacy of the Romans extends beyond objects in museums, books and ruined structures like Hadrian's Wall, impressive as they are. The Fosse Way has passed the test of time and has survived above all because it can still be used.

Lincoln
Lindum Colonia

Leicester
Ratae Corieltauvorum

High Cross
Venonae

Cirencester
Corinium Dobunnorum

Bath
Aquae Sulis

Ilchester
Lindinis

Exeter
Isca Dumnoniorum

Scrooby Manor

NOTTINGHAMSHIRE

Most British people have not heard of Scrooby Manor in northern Nottinghamshire. Scrooby is an unassuming place, not remarkable for its architecture, and not on the tourist trail. But what happened there in the 1590s and early 1600s had repercussions all over the world because it was one of the places where the European colonisation of North America began.

Scrooby was home to William Brewster, whose father, also called William, worked as bailiff for the Archbishop of York, who owned Scrooby Manor. The younger William was educated at Cambridge. One of the burning issues in the university in the late 16th century was reform of the English church. William Brewster would have encountered many men in Cambridge who wanted to transform religious worship, doing away with the Anglican hierarchy and concentrating more closely on the teachings of the Bible. Many of these reformers were Puritans, who wanted to change the church from within. However, some went further, believing it best to break away from the church and worship independently; this group were known as separatists.

Brewster was probably already sympathetic to the reformists when he went to the Netherlands in the 1580s, in the service of the official and diplomat William Davison, who was tasked with negotiating an alliance between England and the Dutch States-General. In the Low Countries, reformed religion was thriving, and Brewster became convinced that he should become a separatist, breaking away from the established church and forming a new congregation, worshipping along reformed lines as people did in Holland.

Back in England in 1606, Brewster formed the Separatist Church of Scrooby, a group of local people who gathered for worship at the manor house. They had to do this in secret because breaking away from the established church was against the law; people could even be punished for not attending weekly services at their local Anglican church. As a result, William Brewster and his brother James found themselves in the ecclesiastical court.

The restrictions on their religious freedom persuaded William and a number of other Scrooby separatists to leave England and settle somewhere where they would be able to worship in their own way. The obvious choice was Holland, where William already had contacts, but even travelling there was difficult, because leaving the country without royal permission was illegal and the separatists were arrested after one attempt. The next time they tried they got away successfully by leaving discreetly from an isolated location in north Lincolnshire. After a brief period in Amsterdam, they settled in Leyden.

In the Low Countries, Brewster made a living running a printing press, producing English religious books that were banned in his home country, but in 1619 his printing type was confiscated as a result of pressure from the English authorities. Not even the Netherlands, it seemed, was a safe haven. This life of persecution and set-back led Brewster and several of the other Scrooby separatists to join the group of 'Pilgrims' sailing on the *Mayflower* in 1620, to start a new life in North America. Brewster became a leading member of the new colony. He was senior elder of the community and a valued adviser to the man they chose as Governor, William Bradford, himself a Nottinghamshire neighbour of the Brewsters.

Brewster and the small community of separatists from Scrooby were at the heart of the history of North America. This is true not just because they founded one of the earliest European colonies but also because of their willingness to stand up for their religious beliefs and the way these beliefs informed their laws and their society. This determination to live well and be directed by the teachings of the Bible helped to shape North America.

Ye Olde Trip to Jerusalem

NOTTINGHAM

Sometimes what makes a place special is not what has survived on the ground or even its history, but the legends and traditions that surround it. This is often the case with pubs and inns, places made attractive and inviting by the feel-good factors of atmosphere, anecdote and myth. No one knows for sure which is the oldest pub in England – several claim to be. One of the best known of these is Nottingham's Ye Olde Trip to Jerusalem, which is said to have been founded in 1189. There is no documentary evidence for this date, but if the pub's date is legendary the building is certainly very old, and, built into the crag below Nottingham Castle, with walls and ceilings of bare rock, it is also very atmospheric. The small white-walled building hunkered against the rock is eye-catching from outside, but within its succession of small, irregularly shaped rooms, some with cave-like walls and ceilings, it is unlike any other pub.

The significance of the date 1189 is that it marks the beginning of the Third Crusade, when forces from across Europe set out to conquer the Holy Land from the Muslim Sultan Saladin; it is also the year in which Richard I, renowned as a crusader, became king. So the inn's name and the date 1189 suggest that it may first have been used as a stopping point for men on their way to fight in the Holy Land. Pilgrims to Jerusalem may also have taken a break there in more peaceful times.

There is evidence that suggests that the caves adjoining the inn were used in the Middle Ages as the brewhouse for the castle above. The brewing of beer was a vital activity in the medieval period. Everyone drank beer because the safety of water supplies was so unreliable, and a brewhouse would have been a key facility in the castle, probably from the very beginning. Brewing on the site could therefore go back to around 1067, when the castle was built. The oldest parts of the pub building itself date to 1650, although a map of 1610 also shows a building nearby. The first documentary record of a pub on the site is in 1751, when it was called The Pilgrim. The use of the current name goes back to 1799.

So the site of Ye Olde Trip to Jerusalem has a long history and the precise age of the pub itself matters less than this. What is important is that it is an ancient part of a long tradition of beer drinking and offering hospitality, especially to travellers, which is what alehouses and pubs have been doing for centuries. In the Middle Ages, when travel was difficult, dangerous and slow, the sight of a pub or inn could offer respite to an exhausted pilgrim, merchant or craftsman. Today, when we travel much more freely and easily, a pub is still welcome – and one as atmospheric, historic and unusual as Ye Olde Trip to Jerusalem is a destination in its own right.

East Side of Caister Camp.

Caister Camp

CAISTER-ON-SEA, NORFOLK

For much of the 20th century holiday camps were a great British institution. Before cheap air travel began to take people on overseas package holidays, millions flocked to camps where they lived for a week or two in wooden chalets and enjoyed a range of entertainment – everything from stand-up comedy to knobby knees competitions – which was all provided on site. The history of this kind of holiday began in the 1890s at places like Cunningham's Young Men's Holiday Camp on the Isle of Man. These were literally camps, where hardy young people turned up for a week under canvas. But one of the first holiday camps with permanent chalets was Caister Camp, at Caister-on-Sea near Great Yarmouth.

Caister Camp began like Cunningham's, with tents. It was the idea of socialist, teetotaller, and former grocer John Fletcher Dodd. The camp began in 1906 when Dodd bought a house at Caister, pitched three bell tents in the garden, and invited some of his socialist friends to stay. Soon Dodd added more tents and the camp became larger and more formal. Most of the guests were socialists; many were members of the Independent Labour Party. In the early days, the majority were working men from East London, but socialist luminaries such as George Bernard Shaw and Kier Hardy also attended.

The camp was run according to strict rules. There was no alcohol, gambling was banned, and a 'no noise after 11 pm' regulation was enforced. The camp was open to families, except those with children under two years of age. There were set meal times announced by the blowing of a bugle, and everyone was expected to turn up promptly for their food. Sleeping in a tent with a straw mattress was hardly luxury, but Dodd's socialist camp gave a lot of poor working people – many of whom had never had a proper holiday – the chance of a week by the sea. The idea proved popular and by 1914 many were paying 21 shillings a week to holiday at Caister.

In the years after World War I the tents were replaced by chalets, together with buildings containing a dining room, newspaper shops, and other facilities. Caister began to look more like the popular image of a holiday camp. It was successful too. There was further expansion and in 1933, Fletcher Dodd even bought 22 tram bodies when Great Yarmouth's trams stopped running and had them converted into extra accommodation. By now the camp was more a business than an idealist venture, and you no longer had to be a socialist to take a holiday there. However, the rules – such as the alcohol and gambling bans and the curfew – remained in place. To these regulations were added others, such as a mandatory camp badge for all residents and the stipulation that visitors had to wear 'the regulation costume' for bathing. None of this deterred visitors, however, and in 1933 the camp even got its own stop on the railway – Caister Camp Halt – a clear signal that it was doing well. By the 1960s, famous names such as Roy Hudd and Ronnie Corbett were being hired to provide the entertainment.

The combination of simple accommodation, on-site entertainment, and a strict regime set the style for British holiday camps. When Billy Butlin opened his first camp in Skegness in 1936 it was run along similar lines. From the 1950s to the 1970s, companies like Butlin's and their rivals Pontin's – together with pioneers such as Caister – were major players in the British holiday market. However, the spread of cheap foreign travel forced a rethink. Companies dropped the word 'camp' with its spartan implications, made their facilities more luxurious, offered more sophisticated entertainment, and rebranded their destinations as 'holiday centres'. But people still remember early holiday camps, pioneered by Fletcher Dodd at Caister, with fondness, as places that brought family holidays to the masses for the first time.

Pump Room and Roman Baths

BATH, SOMERSET

Nowhere in England is more steeped in the history of travel and tourism than the city of Bath. People came here to take advantage of the health-giving waters supplied by three geothermal springs in the ancient British and Roman periods; Bath was a major spa and resort in the 18th century; today it is still one of the most popular tourist destinations in the country. Modern visitors are drawn by the long history of the place and its array of beautiful old buildings, and the most evocative of these are the Roman baths and the pump rooms of the Georgian era.

When the Romans came to the area in the 1st century, they merged the cult of the Celtic goddess Sul with their own near-equivalent Minerva, and called the place Aquae Sulis after her. Over several centuries of occupation they built and extended the city's bath complex to create a series of heated rooms and pools near the temple of Sulis-Minerva. The Romans bathed by progressing through a number of rooms, starting in the frigidarium or cold room, going on to the warmer tepidarium, before entering the caldarium or hot room. Having built up a sweat, they went to a cold room where they had a massage and a scraping with metal implements to remove massage oil, perspiration and dirt.

By the 4th century the bath complex was very large – Bath was a major settlement and Roman bath houses were social centres, where people met friends and business colleagues. A large part of the complex still remains, partly sheltered by 18th- and 19th-century walls and roofs. Visitors can see the large lead-lined Great Bath, flanked on either side by the East and West ranges, each of which contains several pools and hot rooms, originally warmed by hot air under the floor. Adjoining these rooms is the spring, sacred to Sulis-Minerva, which supplies 240,000 gallons of mineral-rich water to the site every day; the water still flows through Roman ducts and drains, filling several of the baths. Thousands of finds from the site are displayed.

After the Roman period, the city's next heyday began when Bath became a fashionable resort in the Georgian period. The town expanded hugely: the population rose from less than 3,000 in 1700 to about 33,000 a century later. The heart of the Georgian spa was the Grand Pump Room. This was built by Thomas Baldwin in 1790–95 and replaced an earlier pump room, constructed at the beginning of the century. The pump room is adjacent to the Roman baths (when the foundations were dug, remains of the Roman temple of Minerva were found) and allowed both bathing and drinking the healing water to take place in separate but nearby places.

In the 18th and 19th centuries the Pump Room was open from 9am to 3pm, and people came to promenade up and down the large saloon, occasionally pausing to drink the hot, mineral-rich water, while a small orchestra in a gallery at one end entertained them. The Pump Room became the social centre of Bath, a place where people would meet friends and strike up new acquaintances.

The Pump Room's Classical design is typical of Georgian Bath. Outside, the façade is dominated by Classical columns and pediments carved with sphinxes; inside pale plaster walls and ceiling, combined with large windows, create a light, pleasant interior that is now home to restaurant tables – though Bath water is still available too. As visitors eat lunch or tea with friends or family, they are doing in 21st-century terms what their Georgian and Roman ancestors did here – visiting and socialising in a sophisticated environment, one that now reflects 2,000 years of the history of travel and tourism in England.

3 Homes and Gardens

Port Sunlight

WIRRAL, MERSEYSIDE

In the 19th century most industrial workers lived in cramped, often insanitary, houses. A few factory owners wanted to change this, and one who did so was the soap manufacturer William Hesketh Lever, who built the garden suburb of Port Sunlight for his workers. By the late 1880s, Lever's business was expanding rapidly. He made a fortune producing soap from vegetable oils and establishing recognisable, trusted brands, such as Sunlight. He needed a bigger factory and decided to move his base from Warrington, Cheshire, to a new site south of the River Mersey, a place he decided to name Port Sunlight after his leading brand. He needed accommodation for the factory's workers too, and the move gave him the opportunity to provide something better than the poor accommodation that most factory workers were forced to endure.

Lever's idea was to build attractive housing in a green setting. There would be proper sanitation, plenty of open space, and facilities galore – sports grounds, parkland, a club, a cottage hospital, schools, and an open-air swimming pool. One thing that made the plan unique was that the houses were laid out on one side of the road only, meaning that the dwellings were not overlooked and that everyone had a view of grass or trees opposite. Another unique feature was that all the houses were different – many were designed by local architects William and Segar Owen, and Grayson and Ould; nationally known architects such as Sir Edwin Lutyens, Sir Ernest George, and Ernest Newton also contributed designs.

The result was a village totally different from the dull, repetitive and unhealthy rows of terraced and back-to-back housing that were common in Britain's industrial towns. The architecture is far from 'industrial'. The houses are in a rich mixture of styles – 'Tudoresque' timber-framing or red brick; 'Queen Anne', with fancy gables and white paintwork; Arts and Crafts, with sweeping rooflines and plain rendered fronts. Buildings like these were a world away from the small, dark, damp houses in many of the towns that led England's industrial revolution. Port Sunlight's grander buildings, such as the later Lady Lever Art Gallery, a memorial to Lever's wife that contains much of the couple's art collection, are in more imposing styles: the gallery is Classical, with a grand portico and shallow dome.

Comfortable, leafy, and visually varied, Port Sunlight was a place where people wanted to live. Lever, a committed Congregationalist, was clearly driven by his beliefs to do well by his employees. But he was also paternalistic – he was convinced that he knew what was best for people – and if he was going to share his profits with his workers, he argued, it was better to do so by housing them well than by giving them more money, which they might squander on rich food or alcohol. In keeping with these views, Port Sunlight's 'pub' at first sold only non-alcoholic drinks, although this policy was later changed after a vote among the residents came down firmly on the side of alcohol.

Lever was not the only Victorian manufacturer who saw the benefits of building decent housing for his workers. He was probably influenced by the work of the textile manufacturer Titus Salt at Saltaire, West Yorkshire. Like Lever, Salt was a Congregationalist and both factory-owners wanted to sweep away the industrial slums and house workers in a way that was comfortable and healthy. But Saltaire, with its uniform rows of brick-built terraced houses, is less architecturally varied than Port Sunlight. It was Port Sunlight (along with Cadbury's Bournville, near Birmingham, which is leafy but less architecturally diverse) that showed the benefits of the true garden village, influencing planners of later garden cities and suburbs for the next few decades. From the leafy suburbs of many English provincial towns to the rows of 1930s Tudoresque houses in areas of outer London, Port Sunlight's influence was widespread and long-lasting.

Royal Horticultural Society Garden

WISLEY, SURREY

The Royal Horticultural Society began in London in 1804. It was originally the Horticultural Society of London and gained its royal charter in 1861. As the country's major gardening charity, it is dedicated to improving and developing all aspects of horticulture. By the late 19th century the RHS had a garden at Chiswick, where it grew plants and held events such as shows and fetes. As the 20th century approached, however, the society realised that it would need more space and started to look for a new garden. The search came to an end when Thomas Hanbury, a businessman who was also a keen gardener, gave his estate at Wisley in Surrey to the society in 1903. Hanbury had bought the Wisley estate the previous year after the death of its previous owner, RHS member George Ferguson Wilson. Wilson had established an experimental garden there, where he developed ways of making difficult plants grow successfully. This garden only occupied part of the 60-acre estate, but it gave the RHS a base on which they could build. Over the following century the RHS made Wisley into one of the world's great gardens and a centre of horticultural research.

Ferguson Wilson's work at Wisley fitted in with the RHS's tradition of experimental gardening, and the trials field, where the RHS gardeners tested new varieties so that they could advise members on which plants to grow, remained the heart of Wisley. Winning the Award of Garden Merit after a plant has been trialled at Wisley is the goal of many growers.

After the RHS acquired Wisley, the garden area expanded, and the trials field was joined by a multitude of new gardens and facilities, from the pinetum, with its now veteran collection of pines, to the rock garden and alpine meadow, from the orchard to specialist wild, walled and other gardens. The area under cultivation now stretches across some 240 acres.

One key facility is the purpose-built laboratory, constructed in 1914–16. This was designed as a base for the society's scientists and for training gardens, so has a lecture room as well as laboratory facilities and a place to store the RHS's large herbarium. It is a beautiful building in the Arts and Crafts style, in a mixture of red brick and timber framing. Its style and setting in front of the Jellicoe Canal recall some of the country houses of Edwin Lutyens.

Development has continued into the 21st century, with the Glasshouse, opened in 2007 to celebrate the bicentenary of the RHS. This structure covers about three-quarters of an acre and its maximum height is 40ft – enough for palms, tree ferns, and other large specimens. The Glasshouse is divided into three zones. The moist temperate zone (8–12°C) accommodates plants such as Australasian tree ferns, South American climbers, and the Ethiopian black banana. The dry temperate zone is home to plants from deserts and semi-arid zones around the world. The tropical zone covers the large-leaved species from the Tropics, including many that are familiar as house plants, but that here grow to their full size.

The RHS Garden at Wisley has grown to become one of the great gardens of the UK. Its beds and model gardens provide glorious vistas and are an inspiration to gardeners, whatever the size and location of their plot. More than this, it carries out important research, testing new varieties and trying out fresh cultivation approaches. Above all, it is about plants – showcasing their qualities, and investigating ways to grow them. In a country where millions of people keep a garden, it is also the centre of a national obsession and part of the British national identity.

Windsor Castle

BERKSHIRE

Medieval fortress, royal residence, centre of ceremony, and the largest occupied castle in the world: Windsor Castle is many things. It has played a central role in English history since 1070, when William I built the first castle at Windsor, and it has since been home to a succession of monarchs, many of whom have altered the building extensively, so that it is now exhibits a fascinating hotchpotch of styles.

Many of the towers and walls visible on the castle's famous skyline originated in the Middle Ages, although all have been altered subsequently – the great Round Tower at the heart of the castle was the work of Henry II in the 1160s and 1170s, the Curfew, Garter and Salisbury Towers and the walls of the Lower Ward were originally built by Henry III in the early 13th century. Edward III did much rebuilding in the 14th century and made the castle the headquarters of his new order of chivalry, the Order of the Garter. St George's Chapel, itself one of the greatest medieval Gothic buildings, was begun by Edward IV in 1475 and completed by Henry VII. The annual Garter service takes place in the chapel, and ten monarchs are buried there.

Most of these medieval buildings were later restored, extended or rebuilt. Charles II added new royal state rooms in the late 17th century, employing the painter Verrio to decorate walls and ceilings; the Queen's Audience and Presence Chambers and the King's Dining Room survive from this period. Much further work was done during the reign of George IV, who employed the architect Jeffry Wyatville. Wyatville added new towers and heightened others, giving the castle the Romantic exterior and skyline it has today. He also remodelled the interiors. The castle therefore represents an interesting mixture of medieval and 19th-century work, with added elements from other periods to create an architectural portrait of the changing tastes and requirements of Britain's rulers.

Under Queen Elizabeth II the castle has been used as a royal residence (the queen spends most weekends there) and for official occasions, including state banquets and receptions, visits of foreign heads of state, and certain royal weddings and funerals. The Round Tower houses the royal archives and photograph collection, while the Print Room and Royal Library are home to an extensive collection of important prints, drawings and manuscripts.

At the same time the castle has become one of the country's most popular tourist attractions, with annual visitor numbers of around 1.3 million. The castle's great age and centuries of use made a repair programme necessary in the late-20th century and it was during repairs in 1992 that a fire began when heat from a spotlight ignited a curtain. The fire spread rapidly to destroy nine of the state rooms and damage more than 100 others. A campaign to repair the building quickly began, with a pragmatic approach adopted in which the rooms were restored close to their pre-fire appearance, reviving traditional crafts but also using modern techniques and materials where these did not affect the appearance of the building. As a result, the castle is now arguably in better shape than it has ever been to withstand the wear and tear of continuous use and large numbers of visitors.

Windsor Castle's history is closely tied to the history of the British monarchy. But it has a wider relevance. Since the Middle Ages, it has been a very large building, a home and workplace for many people, a centre of statesmanship, and a meeting place of dignitaries. The oldest, biggest, and probably best-loved of the British royal residences, it is also a national symbol.

Blenheim Palace

WOODSTOCK, OXFORDSHIRE

A vast baroque palace set by a lake in a stunning landscape garden, Blenheim would stand out in any list of historic houses. It owes its existence to the career of John Churchill, 1st Duke of Marlborough, a national hero of the late Stuart period. John Churchill was the most successful British military leader and statesman of his generation. He had a long career, stretching from the reigns of James II to Queen Anne, and was particularly close to the last Stuart queen because his wife, Sarah, was Anne's closest friend. Marlborough's greatest triumphs came as the leader of British forces in the War of the Spanish Succession, winning famous victories at Blenheim, Ramillies, Oudenarde and Malplaquet in the first decade of the 18th century. Having been made Earl of Marlborough by William and Mary in 1689, he was raised to the dukedom in 1703. As a reward for his further successes in the war, the queen granted him lands near Woodstock, together with money to build himself a magnificent country house.

Marlborough chose as his architect Sir John Vanbrugh, going against the wishes of his wife, who favoured Sir Christopher Wren. Vanbrugh's style was baroque, and he employed it on a grand scale. The house is enormous, with a massive central block containing the state rooms, and two vast flanking courtyards, one for stables, the other housing the kitchen, bakehouse, and other service rooms. Everything, from the colossal columns of the portico to the gargantuan chimneys and finials on the skyline, is on a huge and theatrical scale – and not surprisingly, as Vanbrugh had been a playwright before turning to architecture.

Inside, the array of state rooms is just as imposing. Visitors enter through the cavernous Great Hall, which gives on to the main range of state rooms along the south front. Many of these are hung with tapestries celebrating Marlborough's victories. To the east is the Long Library, a single room occupying one entire side of the house, with enough space for a collection of some 10,000 books. The enormous scale of all this became a problem for the duke and duchess. Sarah disliked Vanbrugh's grand style and quarrelled with him. Things became still more fraught because no precise budget had been agreed with the crown and payments were slow in coming. Further disagreements led to the temporary exile of the duke and duchess, the alienation of Vanbrugh and many of his craftsmen, and the eventual completion of the house by a team under Vanbrugh's assistant, Nicholas Hawksmoor.

The palace that emerged is a tour de force: both a unique memorial to Marlborough and Vanbrugh's masterpiece. It is still more impressive because of its setting. The landscape garden surrounding the house was a later creation, the work of Lancelot 'Capability' Brown, who was employed by the 4th Duke in 1764. Brown's work was on a scale similar to Vanbrugh's. He redesigned the whole landscape around the palace, planting trees, introducing slopes, and damming the River Glyme to produce the enormous lake. The formal gardens close to the house were added in the early 20th century.

It is fitting that this huge house is known as a palace – a word otherwise used in England for houses of the monarch and of bishops of the Church of England. But Blenheim is bigger than most of these other palaces. When George III visited with Queen Charlotte in 1786 he grasped this immediately. 'We have nothing to equal this,' he said.

Blenheim is unique as a British ducal palace, as the greatest work of Vanbrugh, for the garden by Capability Brown, and as the grandest English country house. It is also important for its family associations: not just for the 1st Duke of Marlborough, but also for his descendant, Winston Churchill, who was born in the house. As Marlborough was a hero in his time, so was Churchill in his, and this magnificent house is a memorial to them both.

Prefabricated bungalows

WAKE GREEN ROAD, MOSELEY, BIRMINGHAM

World War II left Britain with a huge housing shortage and before the war ended, the government was laying plans to remedy this by building a large number of new homes. Lord Portal, Minister of Works, devised a scheme to produce prefabricated dwellings to meet the need quickly. These homes were designed to last about a decade, and to act as a temporary stopgap until more conventional houses could be built. But a few are still in use, providing much-loved homes and a valuable record of a turning-point in 20th-century history.

Prefabrication was chosen for several reasons. Speed of construction was key: once the ground was prepared and a foundation laid, a team could erect a prefabricated house in a matter of days or even hours. Bricklayers and carpenters were not required – an advantage because there was a shortage of skilled workers after the war. In addition, prefabs could be produced with fitted bathrooms and kitchens that were installed at the factory, meaning that there was no need for on-site plumbers.

The government laid down a basic specification, covering the size of the accommodation required (a minimum of 635 square feet) and the fitted services. Commercial companies came up with a number of different designs using a range of building materials.

A number of these designs went into production in 1945, but in the event only 156,623 prefabs were built. The main reason was money. A temporary bungalow cost a similar amount to produce as a conventional, brick-built house. In spite of the prefabs' modern design and facilities, and their popularity with residents, the programme was shelved.

Most of the post-war prefabs lasted a good deal longer than 10 years, but now, over 70 years after the end of the war, most have been demolished and their sites reused to build flats and houses at much greater density. Of the few that remain, the 16 steel-framed Phoenix bungalows in Wake Green Road, Moseley, Birmingham, have survived well enough to be given Grade II listed status. They are clad with corrugated asbestos sheeting and a felt-covered asbestos roof. The interior walls are clad with timber. Each has two bedrooms and features the standard 'service core', a unit containing the kitchen and bathroom, both fully fitted.

The prefabs were popular with residents. They were detached at a time when most people were living in terraced or semi-detached houses, and each had its own garden. The modern, fitted interiors were completely unlike anything most people had seen and offered far better facilities than the basic kitchens and tin baths that many working-class families had put up with for years.

Prefabs proved surprisingly durable: many lasted for decades and they were often well looked after by appreciative tenants. However, some eventually developed problems with rot and rust, and the fact that some designs, including the Phoenix, included asbestos, meant potential health hazards. Councils, realising that they could provide more housing units per acre by building over the gardens, demolished most of them. Only a handful now remain. They are important as rare survivals of an unusual housing type that retain many of their original features, and as reminders of a point in British history, when the country emerged from war and began to rebuild, creating homes that were fit for modern life.

Free Gardens and Allotments

GREAT SOMERFORD, WILTSHIRE

England has thousands of allotments, and they are as popular as ever. But few of the enthusiastic gardeners who cultivate them know that the modern allotment movement began over 200 years ago in Great Somerford, Wiltshire, where people still grow produce on the plots tilled by their pioneer ancestors.

Allotments as we know them today have their roots in a practice that transformed land use in England: enclosure. This was the process by which landowners enclosed or fenced off rural farm land, dividing up the old open fields and common land. The rural poor had relied on these lands, especially the commons, which were used principally to graze animals, but also sometimes as a source of wood or turf for fuel, or as a place where pigs could forage for beech mast or other nuts. Enclosure made many people landless and without the means to produce their own food. This happened at different times in different places. There was some enclosure in the Middle Ages, some in Tudor times, and there were more and more enclosures in the 17th and 18th centuries, with each place requiring its own act of parliament. The practice reached a peak in the 19th century, after Parliament passed General Enclosure Acts in 1836 and 1840, allowing enclosure without further parliamentary approval.

In some areas, however, benevolent landlords and individuals stepped in to help the poor. This is what happened in Great Somerford. Some of the land here was enclosed in the 17th century, but the remaining open fields and commons were enclosed in 1809. This was when the village's rector, Stephen Demainbray, petitioned King George III to allow land south of the village to be set aside as allotments for the village people. The allotments remain and are probably the oldest in continuous cultivation.

The village was fortunate in having Demainbray as rector because he was a philanthropist with royal connections – he was chaplain to George III, so had the king's ear. He had seen what a neighbour, Thomas Estcourt of Shipton Moyne in Gloucestershire, had achieved by renting small parcels of land to the poor: people were able to grow sufficient food and very few people in Estcourt's village had to ask for poor relief. So when Great Somerford's Enclosure Act was passed by Parliament, it included a clause requiring land to be set aside for the landless poor.

Initially a six-acre site was provided for the people of Great Somerford, who originally grew wheat, oats, potatoes, and other vegetables, together with mangel wurzels as fodder for livestock. Every year, on the Tuesday after Easter Sunday, the allotments were inspected and the tenants' contracts renewed. The allotments are still well used. There are now 50, and they are free to local residents. Allotment-holders, some of whom have kept their allotments for many decades, grow a range of produce.

Parliament also passed acts that required 'field gardens' to be provided for the landless poor when enclosures were made in other places, but few such gardens or allotments were actually provided until a further law in 1887 required local authorities to set them up. So the allotment gardeners at Great Somerford were among a few isolated pioneers until the late Victorian period. But with more and more allotments being established in the late 19th and early 20th centuries, the allotment movement grew to its present size. There are now around 300,000 council-owned allotments in Britain and a further substantial number on private land or created by charities. They remain very popular (with long waiting lists for plots) and help people build a connection with the land and grow healthy, nutritious food. The roots of this vibrant national movement first took hold at the allotments and free gardens of Great Somerford.

Osborne House

ISLE OF WIGHT

Britain's major royal residences, from Buckingham Palace to Windsor Castle, are world famous, but Osborne House on the Isle of Wight is less well known, and is a different kind of building. It is not a palace or a castle, but a family house, built as much for privacy and relaxation as for grand ceremonial occasions. Its history as a royal home began in the 1840s, when Queen Victoria and Prince Albert were looking for a residence by the sea where they and their growing young family could escape from the pressures of court life in London and Windsor. The Prime Minister, Sir Robert Peel, told them that Osborne House on the Isle of Wight was available.

When Albert looked at the house, he realised that it would need to be expanded to meet the demands of a royal couple with a large family and household. He was deeply interested in architecture and, rather than employ an architect in the usual way, consulted the builder Thomas Cubitt, who had developed the Westminster estate in London, for advice. Albert and Cubitt decided to demolish the old house and start again, jointly designing the new building.

By 1851 a striking new house in the Italian Renaissance revival style had emerged, with two tall square towers like campaniles, and other Italianate touches, such as the round-headed windows and broad overhanging cornices. The structure is of brick, but it is finished in pale stucco, just like the streets of terraced houses that Cubitt had built in central London. The house overlooks terraces with the pergolas, pools, statuary and formally arranged beds of an Italian garden. The house itself looks large, but it is not monumental, because it is divided into several distinct and asymmetrically arranged wings.

The house as Albert built it was in three parts. The Pavilion is the heart of the house, with the dining room, drawing room and billiard room on the ground floor, the queen and prince's private rooms on the first floor, and the nursery on the floor above. This part of Osborne was completed first. Next came the sections that turned this family home into a royal residence that could accommodate a sizeable staff and visiting foreign dignitaries: the Main Wing, containing the audience hall and council chamber, and the Household Wing. These are linked to the Pavilion by the imposing Grand Corridor.

The style of Osborne proved very influential. Italianate houses were already being built in Britain when Osborne was begun, but the royal family's adoption of the style made it much more popular, and many quite modest houses were built with stucco façades, round-headed windows, and even towers, in imitation of Osborne. Italianate 'villas', suburban detached houses often with square towers became popular across the entire empire.

After Albert died in 1861, the queen made further additions. She added the Durbar wing in 1890–92 to provide more space for large events. Its main room, the Durbar Room, was used for banquets or receptions. It is highly ornate, decorated with plaster and carton pierre (a version of paper mâché) in a mixture of Mughal and Hindu styles, to reflect the queen's role as head of the British Empire and Empress of India.

The queen continued to use Osborne for the rest of her life, finally dying in the house in 1901. Her son and successor Edward VII did not want Osborne, so gave the house to the state, on the condition that his parents' private rooms were preserved and sealed off. In the early 20th century, Osborne was a convalescent home for officers, and a naval college was built in the grounds. Then the house was let to various private tenants until in 1954 Queen Elizabeth II gave permission for the house (including the royal apartments) to be opened to the public. Osborne has remained a popular visitor destination ever since, valued especially for the unique insight it gives into the life and taste of one of the country's longest-reigning monarchs.

Hospital of St Cross

WINCHESTER, HAMPSHIRE

Before the welfare state, social housing, and the existence of widespread charitable support, what happened to those who were too ill or too old to work? In many cases, the person's family gave what help they could, but there was not always a family, or they might themselves be poor. In the Middle Ages a few people – typically under the auspices of the church – addressed this issue by setting up charitable almshouses in which the poor or infirm could be housed. One of these is the Hospital of St Cross in Winchester, founded in the 1130s and laid out around stone-built quadrangles planted with lawns and shrubs. It is still fulfilling the same function today and is said to be the oldest charitable institution in Britain.

The Hospital of St Cross was founded by Henry of Blois, Bishop of Winchester and grandson of King William I. According to legend, Henry founded the hospital after he met a poor young woman when he was walking in the Itchen Meadows. She begged him to help the local people, who were starving because of the civil war. When his walk took him past a ruined monastery, he made a vow to found a new institution to help the poor. The result was the Hospital of St Cross, which he set up to house 13 infirm old men who could not work. In addition, the hospital was to give food to 100 men at the gates every day.

The hospital's church, where residents attend daily prayers, is largely 12th and 13th century. It is built on a grand scale – spacious and tall, with stone vaulted roofs and walls about a metre thick. This building alone is a precious survival of medieval architecture on a scale approaching that of a cathedral or large abbey church. Its solid architectural forms, typical of the transition period between thick-walled round-arched Norman and more delicate pointed-arched Gothic styles, is dignified and imposing.

The hospital is arranged around two quadrangles, designed rather like those of Oxford or Cambridge colleges. Most of the buildings, which include accommodation for the residents, a large hall, kitchen, brewhouse and master's lodgings, are later than the hospital's foundation; they date to various rebuildings and extensions between the 14th and 16th centuries. Many of the additions date to the time when Henry Beaufort was bishop of Winchester. Beaufort was adviser to several kings and was appointed cardinal by Pope Martin V in 1426.

The hospital was not England's first almshouse – records show that almshouses were in existence before the Norman conquest. But it is the oldest one to survive today, and it still operates along the lines laid down by Henry of Blois and his successor Henry Beaufort. This, together with its unique collection of medieval buildings, makes it a very special survival indeed. However, its significance goes beyond this. The hospital set the style for countless later almshouses, which provided shelter and food for the old and infirm for hundreds of years. From the medieval period to the Victorian age, they were the main source of social housing until the arrival of the welfare state in the 20th century. St Cross and the charities that came after it have helped millions of people in need.

Park Hill

SHEFFIELD

By the mid-1950s, the destruction brought by World War II, combined with the baby boom and the need to replace poor, dilapidated Victorian housing, had created a pressing demand for new housing in Britain's towns and cities. By this time, technology had made high-rise structures straightforward to build from concrete and steel, and many of the developments put up to meet the new need were large blocks of flats. The block at Park Hill in Sheffield is vast, packing in 995 homes in a sprawling structure made up of a series of wings connected by bridges. It was the brainchild of architects Jack Lynn and Ivor Smith, working under the City Architect J L Womersley. The exposed structural frame of the building is concrete, with coloured brick curtain walls and the bold, forceful architectural style is what has come to be known as Brutalism.

Uncompromising, stark and minimally decorated, Brutalist buildings have been criticised as harsh and inhuman. When Park Hill was built, however, the view was rather different. Although the complex looked immense and crag-like from a distance, up close it was not inhuman at all. It was made up of modern, well-equipped flats that were much better than the houses they replaced. Many of the houses had neither running water nor mains drainage. The new flats had modern facilities and sanitation, and were spacious, light and airy. They were surrounded by greenery and set well away from noisy, polluted streets.

The development was also designed as a community. Previously, there had been a lot of street-level contact between neighbours and their children. Mindful of existing ties and friendships, the council rehoused neighbours next to one another. The old city streets were not just thoroughfares, they were meeting places and play areas. The architects sought to replicate this by building 'streets in the sky' connecting the flats. Front doors opened onto broad aerial walkways or 'street decks' with views across the green space, where people could meet, talk and play. These street decks were so wide that even the milkman's float could drive along them. A doctors' surgery, a nursery, 31 shops and three pubs were also built into the scheme.

The development uses the site to advantage too. The ground slopes considerably, and the blocks vary in height while maintaining the same roof level. The sloping ground also means that all except the uppermost access deck can reach ground level at some point. This integrates the structure into the hillside while also emphasising its craggy appearance, which perhaps recalls the quarries that used to occupy part of the site.

The positive aspects of the Park Hill scheme – its up-to-date architectural style, its use of the sloping site, and its thoughtful provision for a true community – were celebrated widely when the estate was completed in 1961. Sheffield Council even produced a booklet on the scheme in several languages, confident that Park Hill would be of interest to architects and planners around the world. In spite of this, the estate did not live up to its promise. Although initially well liked, Park Hill deteriorated both architecturally (it was poorly maintained) and socially (the streets in the sky became home to crime rather than community). By the 1990s, it had become hard to find tenants and many of the flats were unoccupied.

However, in 1998 Park Hill was listed at grade II* for its groundbreaking architecture, which makes it a landmark in the history of social housing. The council hoped that this would attract investment to the estate and lead to restoration, but it took until 2009 for a restoration scheme by the developer Urban Splash to get underway. It is planned to have the whole estate renovated by 2022. This scheme involves privatising many of the flats, leaving some 200 for social rent, but the unique architecture of Park Hill will be preserved.

Birkenhead Park

MERSEYSIDE

In the 19th century, the idea of green spaces in cities was not new, but much of this space was privately owned. In London, for example, the royal parks were only opened to the public in the 19th century. Green Park, for example, opened to the public in 1826 and the newly developed Regent's Park was opened two days a week in 1835. However, in many towns, especially those that were expanding rapidly with the rise of industry in the 19th century, there was little or no green space. One influential park, in Birkenhead, led the way in changing this, making pleasant, publicly owned green space a reality in Britain's towns and cities.

The idea for a public park in Birkenhead came from the town's Improvement Commissioners, whose work normally involved providing public facilities such as street paving and lighting. In 1841, Birkenhead's commissioners came up with the idea of a municipally owned park and an Act of Parliament was passed to allow them to use public money to buy a tract of land on the western edge of the town. They parcelled off plots on the edge of the site, so that they could build houses to sell to fund the creation of the park on the remaining area.

Joseph Paxton was hired as the park's designer. It was a good choice: Paxton had had a successful career designing and running the gardens at the Duke of Devonshire's country house at Chatsworth, Derbyshire. At Chatsworth, where he was appointed head gardener at the age of 20, he redesigned part of the garden, built the famous Emperor Fountain, and designed the conservatory (known as the 'Great Stove'), an enormous greenhouse that was then the largest glass structure in the world. He had also designed Liverpool's Prince's Park, a private development but open to the public.

Birkenhead Park was a large-scale project. The total area including the plots for houses was 226 acres, and much of the ground was marshy and needed draining. There followed extensive earth-moving work to create mounds, terraces, lakes and rockeries. Then a campaign of laying out paths and roads, and adding plants, trees and shrubs began. The whole process took some five years.

By the time the park opened in 1847, Paxton had created two distinct areas, the upper and lower park, each with a lake, areas of intensive planting, and contrasting areas given over mainly to grass. The parts of the park were connected by both footpaths and carriage drives, and punctuated by buildings such as the 'Swiss bridge' and a lakeside structure that combined the roles of bandstand and boathouse. Around the edge of the development, the park's presence was signalled with five entrances with lodges.

As well as being very popular in Birkenhead, the park gained many admirers from further afield. It influenced Liverpool's Sefton Park and soon many other English towns were following suit as people came to recognise the benefit of open space and fresh air. Three years after the park opened, the American landscape artist Frederick Law Olmstead paid a visit. He praised its designer for 'the manner in which art had been employed to obtain from nature so much beauty'. America had nothing to compare to it, thought Olmstead. But it is believed that when he won the competition to design New York's Central Park, Birkenhead Park was a major influence on his work. Paxton's park, so transformative for Birkenhead and so influential in Britain, may also have an international significance.

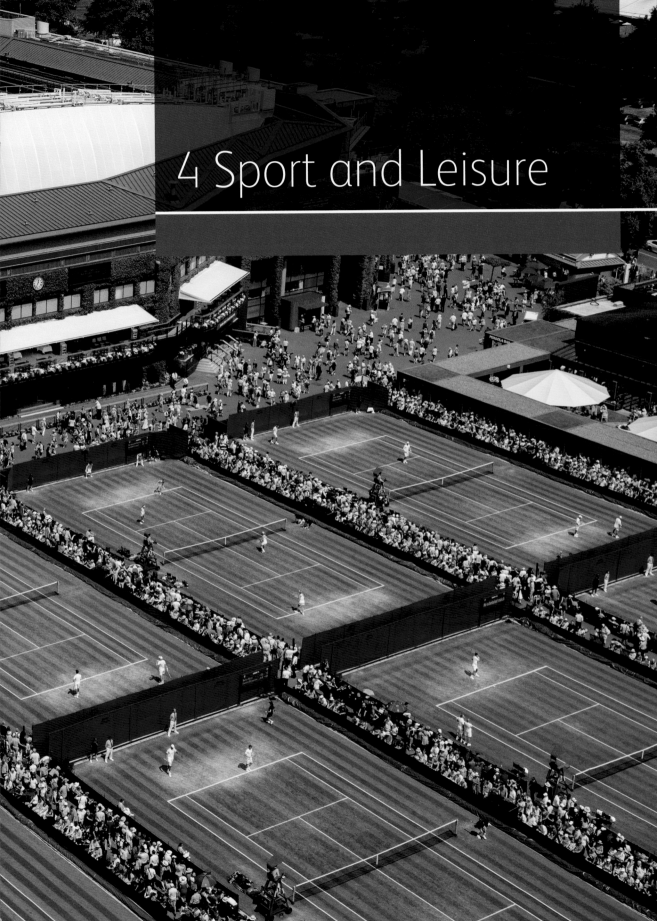

4 Sport and Leisure

Queen Elizabeth Olympic Park
STRATFORD, LONDON

The Queen Elizabeth Olympic Park is one of the most remarkable recent developments in London. It came into being as the setting for the 2012 Summer Olympics and Paralympics, and has a place in sporting history as the scene of one of the most successful games of recent times. However, the original Olympic bid stressed the importance of the legacy of the games and this was not only the historical legacy of memories and medals, nor just the influence of the games on the development of sports in Britain; the plan was that the park and Olympic Village should survive at least in part, and have a major long-term role.

The park consists of 560 acres of land in London's Lea Valley area. This was transformed for the games from a mixture of run-down streets, contaminated industrial land and riverside areas. Numerous venues were built, of which four key ones were designed to be permanent. These are the London Aquatics Centre, with its sweeping curved roof sheltering two 50m pools and a 25m diving pool, designed by Zaha Hadid; the London Stadium, originally home to the Olympic track and field events and now tenanted by West Ham FC and UK Athletics, designed by Populous; the multisport Copper Box Arena, designed by Make Architects; and the Lea Valley Velo Park, by Hopkins Architects. In addition, the park is home to the ArcelorMittal Orbit, a combination of observation tower, sculpture and slide, created by sculptor Sir Anish Kapoor and engineer Cecil Balmond. More than 20 other public artworks enhance the site. Neighbouring the park area is the East Village, built for the Olympic Athletes and now a residential district with housing and shops. The stadia and allied buildings are set in a landscaped park encompassing a large part of the area used for the games.

As well as providing this impressive array of sporting and leisure facilities, this huge urban park – one of the largest created anywhere in the last 150 years – accommodates headquarters for Transport for London, and there are plans for other organisations to be based there. At the heart of all this development, the wetland habitat of the valley has been restored and there are allotments for local people.

None of this has been created without controversy. The construction of the park involved much disruption of existing communities and destruction of old, if run-down cityscape – not everyone saw this as replacing urban dereliction. The design of the park, with its abundance of large hard-surfaced gathering areas that were necessary for the Olympics (and remain useful for major events in the London Stadium) does not please everyone.

However, the four surviving Olympic venues are well liked, especially the Aquatics Centre, where the removal of the temporary seating required for the Olympics now allows the stunning roof to be fully appreciated, and the Copper Box, with its smaller versatile space and striking metallic skin. Venues like these and the main stadium will always attract users and will play their part in ensuring that the sporting legacy of the games will have a fitting setting. The park is a triumph compared with the urban decay on former Olympic sites in some other cities. The planting is also coming into its own – both the 4,300 new trees and the many native species planted to enhance wildlife habitats. The Queen Elizabeth Olympic Park, a project of surprising daring during a challenging period of Britain's economic history, is not only a memento of the remarkable 2012 games, but is also a gesture of hope for the future.

Aintree Racecourse

LIVERPOOL

Horse racing has a long history in Liverpool. It goes back at least to the 18th century, when there were races across the sands at Crosby. Racing at Aintree began in 1829, when William Lynn, landlord of Aintree's Waterloo Hotel, created a racecourse next door. In 1836 he built a new grandstand and staged a four-mile steeplechase, which was won by Captain Martin Becher on The Duke: this is the origin of the Grand National race, although the famous name had not yet been coined, and the beginning of Aintree's history as one of the best loved race courses in the world. The following year, Becher entered the race again, but this time he fell. The fence where he was unhorsed was named Becher's Brook in his honour.

In the next few years, the steeplechases at Aintree became increasingly popular. The course became better organised, and the railway arrived in Liverpool, helping to increase attendances. By 1839 the standard of runners and riders was high, there was a large crowd, and the press were there to report the results. The main event, the Grand Liverpool Steeplechase, was won that year by a horse called Lottery, and horse and rider had to overcome obstacles such as a stone wall and a ploughed field. A newspaper report described the race as 'national', and the name 'Grand National' stuck. 1839 is generally accepted as the first year the Grand National was run.

The original Grand National races were cross-country steeplechases – in other words they were run partly on the course itself, partly across adjoining countryside, clearing obstacles, such as hedges, gates, and a brook, that were already there. Eventually, some of this countryside was incorporated into the racecourse itself, and the National Course now has 16 large and challenging fences, 14 of which are jumped twice. These were originally built of solid wooden cores covered with branches of spruce, added loosely on top of the fences so that the horses can knock these off as they jump, hopefully avoiding contact with the more solid and dangerous core beneath.

The National fences are high and require both skill and stamina to clear. Some are famous, and command respect – even fear – among riders and trainers. Becher's Brook is a 5-foot-high fence which is lower on the landing side than the take-off side – often fooling runners. Canal Turn has a tricky 90-degree turn immediately after the fence – miss it, and the Leeds and Liverpool Canal is dauntingly close. The Chair has a 6-foot-wide ditch followed by the highest fence on the course, a monster of 5 feet 2 inches. There have been many mishaps on these tough fences, some of them serious, and the Grand National has been controversial for the number of damaging falls, some of which have led to horses being put down. In response to these concerns, the fence cores are now made of a plastic material that is more flexible than the old wooden cores.

The unique National course has seen some of racing's most memorable achievements. Perhaps most famous were those of three-times winner Red Rum. No horse has done better at Aintree, but every winner on the National course has managed one of the greatest feats in racing. Aintree is not just about the Grand National. As well as the formidable National course, the site houses the less challenging Mildmay course, which has more conventional National Hunt fences and hurdles. In addition, there is the Aintree Motor Racing Circuit. This was added in 1954 and hosted the British Formula One Grand Prix five times in the 1950s and 1960s; it now hosts a range of car and motorcycle races. These events bring more spectators, interest and revenue to Aintree. But the unique spectacle of the Grand National is what has made the place famous for more than 170 years.

Tower Ballroom

BLACKPOOL, LANCASHIRE

Like many Victorian coastal towns, Blackpool became a popular seaside resort in the decades after the railway boom of the 1840s. By the 1880s, Blackpool had expanded hugely and was offering visitors piers, pubs, fish and chip shops, and donkey rides. Transport through the town was made easy by the famous trams. Blackpool was fast becoming the most popular seaside resort in northern England.

In 1891, shares in the Blackpool Tower Company went on sale. The aim of the company was to build a new visitor attraction for the town: a replica of the Eiffel Tower. The idea came from Blackpool's mayor, John Bickerstaffe, who had visited Paris and admired the Eiffel Tower. Blackpool's version was designed to incorporate an observation platform, a circus, and a ballroom to create a kind of vertical pleasure pier that would become the most famous seaside building in the country.

Three years later, the tower opened. Thousands turned up, paid sixpence to get in and another sixpence to take the lifts to the top. However, the tower's small ballroom was soon eclipsed by the Empress Ballroom, which opened in the town's Winter Gardens in 1896. At 12,500 square feet, this was one of the largest ballrooms in the world, and was very luxuriously decorated. The Tower's owners decided to up their game, and hired the great theatre architect Frank Matcham (designer of some of the country's largest and most opulent venues, such as London's Coliseum Theatre) to design a new ballroom.

Opened in 1899, Matcham's new ballroom was a triumph. It was spacious, lined with balconies from which people could watch the dancing, and luxuriously decorated in the most elaborate Baroque style, with ceiling paintings, ornate plasterwork, gilding, and glittering lights. Winged caryatids, cherubs, scrollwork and onion domes above some of the boxes add to the lavish effect. Most importantly the ballroom was fitted with a large sprung dance floor 120 feet square and made of 30,602 blocks of hardwood. The opulent decoration and the sprung floor attracted dancers in their thousands and the ballroom justified its larger capacity – up to 2,500, depending on the event. Much of the attraction was the sheer glamour of the place: working-class visitors from a Lancashire mill town could feel they had moved up several social classes.

Until well after World War II, Blackpool was the best known seaside holiday town in Britain and one of the most popular. The tower – lit up at night or standing proud by day – was its most famous landmark, and the ballroom made it the most popular destination too. After 1930, the music for dancing in the ballroom usually came from a large Wurlitzer organ, with renowned musician Reginald Dixon at the console. Dixon presided for 40 years, designing a new improved organ in 1935 and seeing the ballroom through the trauma of a fire in 1956. Before he retired in 1970 the place had become one of the settings for the BBC's popular ballroom dancing show *Come Dancing*. It has also been the venue for the show's successor, *Strictly Come Dancing*.

By the 1980s, with the rise of inexpensive air travel and package holidays, English seaside resorts became less popular and less prosperous than they had been before World War II. In Blackpool's case, the decline was accelerated by the closure of many textile factories in northern England, whose workers had made up a large number of Blackpool's summer visitors.

However, many people still visit – often taking advantage of the motorway network to make a day-trip rather than an extended stay. And the publicity brought from the television appearances has helped keep the Tower Ballroom in the public eye. It survives as one of the best interiors by a notable architect and as a symbol of countless Blackpool holidays, made special by the chance to dance in the ballroom's uniquely opulent and glamorous atmosphere.

The All England Lawn Tennis and Croquet Club

CHURCH ROAD, WIMBLEDON, LONDON

For many people, Wimbledon is the essence of the British summer. A top-level sporting tournament in which some of the world's greatest athletes compete in a near-perfect arena; a game that combines fast-moving drama with endurance; an occasion that forms a highlight of the world sporting calendar for players and spectators alike: The Championships, Wimbledon, is all these things. The event has become a unique and valued part of Britain's heritage.

And yet lawn tennis is not an ancient game. Its rules were first officially written down in the 1870s, and in 1877 the first Championships was played at the grounds of the All England Croquet Club in Worple Road, Wimbledon. Only Gentlemen's singles was played, and just 22 people entered, of whom 21 actually turned up. The Club changed its name to the All England Croquet and Lawn Tennis Club for the occasion, and a tradition was born. To begin with, Wimbledon was low-key. Ladies' Singles and Gentlemen's Doubles matches were added in 1884, with Ladies' Doubles and Mixed Doubles appearing in 1913.

In the early 1920s lawn tennis became much more popular, largely as a result of the great French player Suzanne Lenglen, who won a string of international tournaments, including six Wimbledon singles trophies in 1919–25, and gained an enormous following. The All England Club realised it needed new premises to accommodate the growing numbers of spectators, and moved to Church Road, Wimbledon, where both the Club and The Championships have been based ever since. The famous Centre Court was built at this time, with the other show courts, numbers 1 and 2, following in 1923–4.

By the mid-1920s, the royal family were attending Wimbledon regularly, The Championships was becoming a much-loved part of the London social calendar, and with the US, French and Australian Championships it was one of four major tournaments known as 'Grand Slams'. Throughout the following decades, the All England Club gradually expanded. More land to the north of the original site was acquired in 1967, extra courts were added, and improved show courts built. Today Wimbledon has 18 Championships courts, 20 practice courts, plus clay, indoor and acrylic courts. The site can accommodate some 39,000 spectators, 15,000 of them in the Centre Court; the total attendance for the tournament is just under 500,000.

Wimbledon's unique features – its history, its outstanding facilities, the fact that it is the only Grand Slam tournament played on grass – make it immensely popular. All of the world's best players can be seen here, and nearly all of them appreciate the uniqueness of the place. To win here, and to have your name next to the greats like Sampras, Borg and Federer, King, Navratilova or the Williams sisters is a pinnacle of achievement, recognised by everyone. Centre Court tickets are at a premium and those who cannot get into the show courts watch the action on the outer courts or make for the Hill, where they can watch show court matches on a large screen.

Facilities like the Hill go some way to make Wimbledon more accessible. If The Championships still has something in common with a very large garden party – 34,000kg of strawberries are consumed in the fortnight, along with 320,000 glasses of Pimm's – it is no longer an exclusive upper-class garden party. It is about combining excellence with enjoyment.

Having hugely improved the site with everything from better facilities for players to the famous retracting roof of the Centre Court, the All England Club plans further developments for the future. They will be building on nearly a century of tradition on the Church Road site, and ensuring that Wimbledon will remain one of the world's outstanding sporting venues for the foreseeable future.

Saltdean Lido

BRIGHTON

In the 1920s and 1930s, swimming became increasingly popular as a pastime. There were several reasons for this. One was the publicity garnered by the various athletes who swam the English Channel. Channel swimming gained a lot of notice in the 1920s because in 1926 Gertrude Ederle became the first woman to swim the Channel, breaking the record by two hours in the process. Several other female Channel swimmers followed before the end of the decade. At the same time, it became more acceptable for women to wear more practical, streamlined swimming costumes as Victorian and Edwardian restrictions surrounding female clothing began to fall away. In addition, more and more people were aware that swimming was good for the health, and it was seen, along with sunbathing and fresh air, as beneficial.

Many people came to the seaside to swim, but sometimes the tide was far out and on some days the authorities declared the sea 'too rough' for swimming. The solution was purpose-built pools or lidos. Lidos provided a fresh-water pool, changing rooms, viewing platforms, and refreshments for swimmers and spectators. They often had diving boards and slides, and many advertised the cleanliness of the water.

Although some of the early lidos were in a restrained Classical style – Georgian revival for the new Georgian era – increasingly in the 1930s they were built in the latest modern or Art Deco style, with white walls, flat roofs, strip windows, and plain metal banister rails like those on board ship. When used in domestic architecture, this style, which lent itself well to light, airy interiors opening on to sunny terraces, was already associated by both architects and clients with the health-giving properties of sunshine and fresh air. It seemed the ideal style for a lido, and the modernistic elegance of lidos became a familiar feature of English seaside resorts, especially on the south coast.

The lido at Saltdean, a suburb of Brighton, is one of the best examples. Designed by Richard Jones, it was built in 1937–38. Its pool is not the largest of its kind – it has room for 500 bathers. Behind is a two-storey, flat-roofed building that curves around the rear of the pool. Its ground floor contains changing rooms; the upper floor features a central cafe that has a semicircular front with a row of windows running all the way around, so that the interior is lit by sunshine for virtually the entire day. On either side of the cafe are decks where people can watch the swimmers below or simply sunbathe. This strong design with its curving window was probably influenced by another Sussex modernist building, the De La War Pavilion at Bexhill-on-Sea, which was finished three years before.

The stripped-down modern architecture, curving white façades, and practical layout all make Saltdean one of the finest English lidos. Even its relatively small size was an advantage in some ways: at least it did not struggle to attract enough swimmers to pay its way, which was the fate of some of the more ambitious seaside pools.

However, the success of Saltdean lido did not last long. Closure during World War II brought different wartime uses, after which the lido was mothballed and its condition gradually deteriorated. It was eventually repaired and reopened, but by 1995, fewer people were using it and it was closed again. Further restoration was completed in June 2017, and Saltdean Lido is appreciated now as much as it was when it opened, a beacon of modernism and a temple of health, in the 1930s.

The Mall

LONDON

Today the Mall is one of London's best known streets but its origins were humble: it began as a field for the game of pall-mall, which was played with a wooden ball and a mallet, rather like croquet but in a long 'alley' with a single hoop at one end. Today, the Mall is home to a sporting event with a much higher profile as the finishing line of the annual London Marathon.

The Mall took its present form at the beginning of the 20th century, when it was transformed into a processional route linking Buckingham Palace with Trafalgar Square (and thus also with Whitehall and the Houses of Parliament). The route was enhanced by the Victoria Memorial in front of the palace, and the Admiralty Arch at the other end of the Mall was part of the development, which was masterminded by the architect Aston Webb, who also created a new façade for Buckingham Palace. The whole scheme was designed to produce a magnificent ceremonial route, on a par with similar processional ways in cities such as Berlin, Vienna and Washington, DC.

In 1994, the Mall found its new role, as the finishing post for the London Marathon. London's marathon was founded by former Olympic champion Chris Brasher and athlete John Disley, who were inspired to start the event after running the New York Marathon in 1979. Brasher wrote an article about his experience for the *Observer*, in which he described the combination of togetherness and exhilaration generated by the event:

> To believe this story you must believe that the human race can be one joyous family, working together, laughing together, achieving the impossible. Last Sunday, 11,532 men and women from 40 countries in the world, assisted by over a million people, laughed, cheered and suffered during the greatest folk festival the world has seen.

In 1981, the first London Marathon was run, attracting 6,747 runners, of whom 6,255 finished the course. The event was an instant success and the following year 90,000 people applied to take part and 18,059 were accepted to run the magnificent 26-mile course that takes in Greenwich, Tower Bridge, the embankment and the Houses of Parliament. The London Marathon was established on the sporting calendar. Since then, the Marathon has expanded, with the first wheelchair races held in 1983 and the field steadily increasing in size. Although there is huge interest in the elite athletes, the crowds that gather along the route are keen to cheer on the thousands of amateur runners, most of whom run to make money for charitable causes, many of them in fancy dress. 2010 saw the biggest field to date, with around 36,000 finishers.

The first London Marathon finished on Constitution Hill, and from 1982 to 1993 the race ended on Westminster Bridge, with the Houses of Parliament in the background. But in 1994 repairs to the bridge forced the organisers to move the finish to the Mall, where it has remained: they had found the ideal finishing point. The great ceremonial way, with its generous space and background of trees and parks, is an ideal place for the event to come to its climax. Crowds gather to cheer on the finishers and encourage them to find the last burst of energy they need to complete the course and the Mall is transformed from a royal processional way to a place of triumph and achievement for tens of thousands. For the runners, it marks the climax of the event. For spectators, it sums up the whole event: a great common effort of stamina and willpower; in the words of Chris Brasher, 'the world's most human race'.

Crucible Theatre

SHEFFIELD

When Sheffield's Crucible Theatre opened in November 1971, it was widely admired. The architectural design, by Renton Howard Wood Associates, strikingly based on a series of octagons, was modern and impressive, and inside there were attractive and interesting spaces for audiences to pass through before they got to the auditorium. But it was the auditorium itself that was outstanding. This part of the theatre was largely the work of Tanya Moisewitch, a theatre designer well known for her work with Dublin's Abbey Theatre, the Old Vic, and other major companies. She had worked with the director Tyrone Guthrie, an advocate of the thrust stage, and this is the kind of stage she specified at the Crucible.

The Crucible's thrust stage protrudes into the auditorium so that the audience, on its steeply banked rows of seats, surrounds it on three sides. So in spite of the fact that the Crucible seats 980, it has an intimate atmosphere, with no audience member more than 60 feet from the stage. The audience sometimes feels even closer to the action in some productions, because as well as entering from backstage, actors can reach the stage via a pair of ramps positioned between the ranks of seats.

In a life of over 40 years, the Crucible has proved to be a versatile space, hosting not just classical and modern plays, but also dance and music performances. However, the event that has brought it most fame is the World Snooker Championship, the premier event in world snooker, which has been held at the Crucible since 1977. Snooker can be a difficult sport to stage, because to appreciate it, everyone in the audience has to be able to see the whole table and the position of every ball. The good sightlines at the Crucible and the short distance between the audience and stage make it ideal for the snooker spectator.

The Crucible has also become a favourite of the players, not only because of the high standard of the match play in the World Championship, but also because the closeness of the audience makes for a unique atmosphere. All the top players have competed here and, from Steve Davis to Steven Henry, Dennis Taylor to Ronnie O'Sullivan, they all speak warmly of the venue and remember the outstanding matches that have taken place at Sheffield, such as Taylor and Davis's famous 1985 'black-ball final' when the outcome of the championship depended on the final ball of the final frame.

Only about 1,000 people see each World Snooker Championship final live. But millions watch the event on television and the Crucible's special atmosphere also comes over on the screen. While the venue allows the camera to concentrate on the play, the raked seating also gives the producer scope, in moments when there is a break in the action, to linger on the audience, and to give viewers an impression of what it is like to be there. It is a winning combination, and has probably made the Crucible better known that any other British provincial theatre.

Stoke Mandeville Hospital

BUCKINGHAMSHIRE

Sport for people with impairment has a long history, going back at least to the 1880s, when sports clubs for deaf people were established in Berlin. In Britain, its early history is closely identified with Stoke Mandeville Hospital, where wheelchair sports were pioneered in the 1940s, and where the Paralympic Games had their origin. The turning point came in 1944, when Dr Ludwig Guttmann opened a new spinal injuries centre at Stoke Mandeville, to treat servicemen and women who had been injured in the war. Sport was initially used to help patients' rehabilitation. An early example was a hybrid of wheelchair polo and hockey, which was first played as an enjoyable mix of recreation and therapy, but soon evolved into a fully competitive sport.

In 1948 London staged the Olympics and to coincide with this, Guttmann organised an archery event, in which 16 men and women competed. This was a success, and Guttmann made the games into an annual event, adding other sports such as wheelchair netball and basketball, which attracted other teams. In 1952 a Dutch team took part, and this marked the beginning of the International Stoke Mandeville Games. More and more overseas teams participated and 1957 was the first year in which athletes from all five continents competed. Rome hosted the Olympics in 1960, and that year Rome also played host to the ninth Stoke Mandeville Games. Welcoming 400 athletes for 23 different countries, these games were both international and organised to coincide with the olympics. They are generally considered to be the first Paralympic Games – the name derives from a combination of the prefix 'par', denoting parallel, and 'olympic'. Paralympics have been staged regularly every four years since then; since 1988 they have generally taken place in the same cities and venues as the Olympics. Equivalent winter games have also been held since 1976.

The games that began at Stoke Mandeville in the 1940s were on a small scale, and basic in their organisation. Athletes had to stay in hospital accommodation and most of the support was provided by hospital staff – mainly nurses and physiotherapists – working extra hours. The original athletes were patients at Stoke Mandeville itself or from the Royal Star and Garter Hospital at Richmond, which had a similar spinal injuries unit, and were paraplegics. However, as the games expanded, they gained better support and organisation. They have also embraced competitors with a range of impairments – those with impaired muscle power, impaired passive range of movement, leg length difference, limb deficiency, short stature, hypertonia, ataxia, athetosis, vision impairment, and intellectual impairment.

Decades of expansion, better funding, and the link with the Olympics have brought an increasingly high profile to disability sport. This began at Stoke Mandeville, with the work of Sir Ludwig Guttmann and the athletes who competed at the first games in 1948. Stoke Mandeville is still a centre for this branch of sport. The Stoke Mandeville Stadium was one of the venues for the 1984 Summer Paralympics, the last such games not to be held in the same place as the Olympics; it is now the National Centre for Disability Sport in England. Stoke Mandeville's key role in disability sport continues.

Lord's Cricket Ground

ST JOHN'S WOOD, LONDON

The world's most celebrated cricket ground is named after Thomas Lord, who set up his first ground in north London in 1787, on land that is now east of Marylebone Station, on the site of today's Dorset Square. The ground was established on behalf of the White Conduit Club, previously based in Islington, which changed its name to the Marylebone Cricket Club (MCC). In 1811, the ground moved to a site 700 yards northwest, and Lord transplanted the original turf at the request of the members. However, the MCC were soon obliged to move again, because Parliament had approved the building of the Regent's Canal across the site. The landlords, the Eyre Estate, offered Lord another parcel of land, slightly further to the north. Lord took up the turf again, and moved to the new site on St John's Wood Road, where the ground has been since 1814.

The MCC quickly became central to the game of cricket. In 1788, it took control of the laws of the game. It was for much of its history the game's governing body and organised international tours in which the England team played. Lord's became a venue for first-class county and international matches: Middlesex first played there in 1877 and test matches came to Lord's in 1884. The ground was soon regarded as the 'home of cricket', a place with a heritage and atmosphere that makes every match played there special.

Lord's and the MCC have a reputation for conservatism. It is not just the weight of cricketing history that they embody. The club, with its roots in a tradition of gentlemen's clubs that goes back to its 18th-century origins, was men-only until 1999. And yet Lord's cricket ground has moved with the times and contains an outstanding collection of buildings of the 19th and 20th centuries. The fine pavilion, which opened in 1890, is a glowing brick and terracotta structure very much of its time. It contains the vast Long Room, 93 feet in length, through which batsmen have to walk on their way to the wicket, passing an intimidating array of portraits of great cricketers. Spacious is the best word for the pavilion: its architect, Thomas Verity, was also a designer of theatres, and knew how to create spaces with good circulation.

The ground's other outstanding buildings date to the late-20th century. The first of these is the 1987 Mound Stand, which is topped by a canopy made of tough, white PVC material so that it looks like a series of festive tents. It is the work of architects Michael Hopkins & Partners. The other new stand, called simply the Grandstand, stretches along most of the northwest side of the ground. This sleek 1998 structure was designed by Nicholas Grimshaw. The Media Centre, designed by the appropriately named Future Systems, is the most forward-looking of all the buildings on the site. It is a semi-monocoque structure, built of aluminium, constructed like the hull of a boat, and put together by boatbuilders. Its curvaceous, pod-like hull is held high above the ground by a pair of 'legs' that contain lift shafts. Its glazed front is designed to give reporters and radio and TV commentators the best view of the pitch.

Like the early Lord's, which had to move from one site to another in its first decades, Lord's today has shown that it is not afraid of change. Its impressive group of buildings make it one of the best places to watch cricket. But everyone – players, spectators, and commentators in the Media Centre – know that the place also carries an unparalleled history. The great players and memorable matches are commemorated not just in peoples' thoughts but also in the Imperial Cricket Memorial Gallery, housed in a former rackets court behind the pavilion. This is the world's oldest sporting museum, and one more reason that the home of cricket is unique.

Twickenham Stadium

LONDON

The world's best known rugby stadium was established at Twickenham in 1907, when the Rugby Football Union bought 10 acres of land west of London and opened their ground there in 1909. It was a risky choice of site – at that point Twickenham was outside London's built-up area, and the ground was not on a bus route; the nearest station was a mile away. Twickenham was an area of market gardens, and the ground nickname, 'the cabbage patch', arose because of this, although the land bought by the RFU had in fact been an orchard.

If it seems an unpromising start, the stadium developed impressively, especially in the 1920s and 1930s, when Twickenham's capacity grew to 74,000, housed in three stands, allowing crowds of unprecedented size for rugby union. The transport problems were gradually solved too: by 1924 buses were stopping nearby and in 1933 Twickenham Bridge was opened, making travel by road easier.

There was a record crowd of 60,000 when England played New Zealand in January 1925, and Twickenham hosted many 'firsts' in the interwar years. From 1927, the year that saw the first BBC outside broadcast and the first Varsity Match, to 1938, when an England–Scotland match was the first to be broadcast live on television, Twickenham was making history, and becoming one of Britain's most celebrated sports venues.

Over the following decades, the ground continued to grow, with more capacity added. But the big change came in the late-1980s, when the RFU decided on a major development, to modernise the ground, add yet more capacity, and extend the space for car parking. It was a long-term project, carried out in stages so that the ground could continue to function, but it suffered a major setback when work had hardly begun. On 15th April 1989, the Hillsborough disaster changed stadium design for good. The redevelopment plan was for a stadium with standing on the lower tier and seating above. Twickenham would now have to be an all-seater stadium.

Between 1989 and 2006, the stadium was rebuilt, with four new stands that at the end of the project fitted together seamlessly to provide seating for 82,000. This makes it the UK's second-largest stadium – only Wembley is bigger. Added facilities include a hotel, a fitness centre, the RFU's offices, and a small theatre. The same architect, Terry Ward, oversaw the entire project, meaning that the result is a unified design. Not everyone likes it: the structure is mainly exposed grey concrete, harking back to the architectural Brutalism of the 1960s and 1970s. But it works, and there are reassuring reminders of Twickenham's history dotted around, such as a memorial to Sir George Rowland Hill, Honorary Secretary of the RFU between 1881 and 1904 and the man whose fierce defence of amateur sport helped bring about the split between rugby union and rugby league. Above all, the 1950 weather vane, depicting Hermes passing a rugby ball, a longstanding symbol of the ground and the game, still presides. There is no mistaking the fact that this is still the 'home of rugby'.

5 Music and Literature

Shakespeare's Birthplace

STRATFORD-UPON-AVON, WARWICKSHIRE

The house where Shakespeare was born in Stratford-upon-Avon attracts visitors from all over the world. However, although Shakespeare was a successful writer in his time, he was not world-famous until long after his death – widespread interest in his plays and his life did not develop until the 18th and 19th centuries. As a result his birthplace, although visited by literary pilgrims such as Sir Walter Scott and Lord Byron, was not internationally known until the Victorian period.

It is not known exactly when the Shakespeare house was built, but the family was living there by 1552. We know this because John Shakespeare, the poet's father, was fined in that year for leaving a midden heap (a pile of rubbish) in the street in front of his home. The Shakespeares were still there in the following decades, so it is virtually certain that the poet was born there, in 1564.

John Shakespeare was a glove maker and a dealer in wool and leather. By the time his third child, William, was born, he was quite prosperous and his house, although far from palatial, was one of the bigger ones in the town centre. It had three rooms on the ground floor: a parlour with a fireplace, a large hall with an open hearth in the middle, and a third room, which may have been where John Shakespeare worked. Well known in the town, John served as an alderman, and held several prominent civic offices, becoming the town's high bailiff in 1568.

Although William worked in the theatre in London, he kept his connections with Stratford, and always had a home there. As the eldest surviving son of his parents, he inherited the Henley Street house when his father died in 1601. By this time he had his own house in the town, so he leased the Henley Street house to a tenant and it became an inn, the Maidenhead, later the Swan and Maidenhead. The building passed through various owners and tenants until the mid-19th century, by which time it was in poor repair, and partly refaced in brick. In 1846 it went on the market and the American showman P T Barnum announced that he planned to buy it, take it apart, and re-erect it in the USA.

In response a Shakespeare Birthday Committee (later the Shakespeare Birthplace Trust) was formed to raise the money needed to buy the house. The committee had the backing of famous writers such as Charles Dickens and was soon successful in raising the money, buying the house, and restoring it. They removed the brick facing and took the building back, as far as the evidence allowed, to how it was in the 16th century. It soon became one of the country's most popular tourist attractions, especially after the creation of the Shakespeare Memorial Theatre in the town made Stratford a centre for the production of Shakespeare's plays.

Today the birthplace is furnished in period style to give a sense of the life of the Shakespeare family when William was young. Next door is the modern Shakespeare Centre, which contains study facilities including a library and reading room, and a venue for conferences. The trust also looks after several other houses associated with the poet – including Mary Arden's Farm (the home of his mother's family) and Anne Hathaway's Cottage (his wife's family home). They all provide context and background to the plays themselves, produced at the newly rebuilt Royal Shakespeare Theatre, making Stratford Britain's greatest place of literary pilgrimage.

Chetham's Library

MANCHESTER

Humphrey Chetham (1580–1653) was a successful merchant who made a fortune selling cloth. He was born in Crumpsall near Manchester and by the 1620s he was using his new-found wealth to buy property in and near Manchester. Chetham wanted to do good with his money, in particular to give poor people the chance to lift themselves out of poverty, and so he became one of the period's educational pioneers, leaving money in his will to provide both a school for 22 poor boys and a library. The library was to be freely open to the public and the librarian should 'require nothing of any man that cometh into the library'. This was very unusual in this period. The best libraries were miles away, in the universities of Oxford and Cambridge. Many noble families also had private libraries, but these were not open to the public.

When Chetham died, it was the task of his executors to find premises, and set the school and library on a sound footing. They bought the medieval College House, which had been constructed for the priests who served at Manchester's collegiate church (which later became the city's cathedral). This complex of buildings was put up in 1421, but was not used for its original purpose after Henry VIII closed the college of priests in 1547. By Chetham's time the buildings had fallen into disrepair – they had been used as a prison and arsenal during the Civil War and subsequently pigs were kept in the yard and in some of the buildings. The structure was restored and converted for the school.

The building also housed the library and a committee of governors or 'foeffees' set about getting the buildings restored and employing a local man, Richard Martinscroft, to fit and furnish the library. They decided to house the books on the first floor, so that they would not be affected by the damp, and by 1655 three of the governors were in touch with a London bookseller, who was supplying them with an impressive collection of books, especially in the subjects of history, theology, law, medicine and science. They also began to acquire manuscripts. When the books arrived they were chained to the bookshelves, in the traditional medieval manner. The medieval buildings of Chetham's Library and School still survive, and in themselves are important because they are the best-preserved medieval college buildings that still stand in Britain. In addition, the library's 17th-century fittings – its panelling, bookcases and stools – are all still in place. Although the bookcases have been heightened to accommodate more volumes, these fittings still preserve the atmosphere and ambiance of a 17th-century library.

Chetham's library was not unique. Records show that Bristol had a library, linked to All Saints' church, in the 15th century, to which free access was allowed at certain times, and a city library was founded in Norwich in 1608. However, Chetham's holds the distinction of surviving today, and it claims to be the oldest public library in the world. It was not until the 19th century that public libraries became common in Britain, and Chetham's bequest to establish one was visionary. In a period when many public libraries are closing, his long-lasting foundation deserves to be known and celebrated as much as ever.

Brontë Parsonage Museum

HAWORTH, WEST YORKSHIRE

In 1820 a young Irish clergyman, Patrick Brontë, arrived in Haworth, a village in the Yorkshire Pennines, to become perpetual curate. He brought with him his wife Maria and their six children, three of whom were to become some of Britain's most famous writers. They made their home in the parsonage, next to St Michael and All Angels' church, where Patrick would preach every week. The Brontës were not well off – perpetual curates had similar duties to vicars or rectors, but usually earned less – and their children were educated mainly at home. They had few friends and the children travelled little – the parsonage, the village of Haworth, and the adjoining moorland made up their world.

By 1825 this world had become still smaller, because Maria Brontë and two of her daughters, Maria and Elizabeth, had died. The remaining Brontë children – Charlotte, Emily, Anne and their brother Branwell – remained close, spending much of their time writing stories and poems about imaginary worlds called Glass Town, Angria, and Gondal. When they were young women, the parsonage remained the home of Charlotte, Emily, and Anne, the place to which they returned between mostly unhappy spells working as teachers and governesses.

The life of the parsonage, where the siblings encouraged and nurtured one another's talent, was the background to the creation of several of the greatest English novels – especially Charlotte's *Jane Eyre*, Anne's *Agnes Grey*, and Emily's *Wuthering Heights*, all of which were published in 1847. These novels, initially issued under the androgynous pseudonyms Currer, Acton, and Ellis Bell, soon made the sisters famous. Their books, especially *Wuthering Heights* and *Jane Eyre*, have been popular ever since. The books are closely associated with Haworth, not just because they were written there, but also because they are partly set in the windswept countryside that surrounds the village.

The house is a large building today, but it has been extended since the Brontës lived there. In their time it was a typical stone-built middle class house of the area. Now the parsonage is a museum and the Brontë family's life and work is celebrated there in exhibitions and displays. Visitors can see the 'children's study', where the siblings worked together on their early writings, Patrick Brontë's study, and the dining room, where the sisters did much of their mature writing. An extension to the house, built by Patrick Brontë's successor, houses the world's largest collection of Brontë books, manuscripts and memorabilia, making the parsonage a centre of scholarship.

The preservation of the parsonage and the presence of the museum there is largely the result of the work and generosity of the Yorkshire industrialist Sir James Roberts. Roberts was born in Haworth and as a boy heard Patrick Brontë preach. He made his money in the Yorkshire textile business and in 1928 he bought the parsonage and gave it to the Brontë Society (one of the world's oldest literary societies), which has run it as a museum ever since. The house has benefitted from other generous donations, including that of Henry Bonnell, an American collector who gave his large Brontë collection to the Society.

The parsonage does not always look the most inviting of houses. It is set next to the graveyard and can seem forbidding in winter light. However, it was a place to which the Brontë sisters were closely attached – where their father nurtured their talent by giving them the run of his library, and where they found refuge from uncongenial work as governesses. Of the various writers' houses preserved as museums, few are as atmospheric as Haworth. Few classic writers, in addition, have the wide appeal of the Brontës, whose works are read and loved all over the world, and uniquely rooted in the atmosphere and setting of their Yorkshire home.

27b Canonbury Square

ISLINGTON, LONDON

Towards the end of June 1944, a German V-1 flying bomb landed in Mortimer Crescent, Kilburn, London, bringing down the ceilings in the flat where the writer George Orwell lived with his wife Eileen, and their adopted baby son Richard. None of them was hurt, but the flat was made uninhabitable, and the Orwells set about rescuing what they could of their belongings from the rubble – including the manuscript of Orwell's latest novel – and finding somewhere else to live. After a few weeks in temporary accommodation they moved into a top-floor flat at 27b Canonbury Square.

Canonbury Square was then in a run-down area of Islington. The house had been built in 1821 as part of a development for the Marquess of Northampton and the terrace on the eastern side of the square of which it forms a part was originally known as Marquess Terrace. The square was one of many developments built in this period as London's role as a mercantile city and capital of an empire grew and there was an increasing demand for middle-class housing not far from the City and West End. However, this pleasant Regency house had now, like many in the area, been converted into flats. It was down at heel, but with wartime London scarred by bombing, it was as good as the hard-working writer could hope for.

Life was hard for Orwell at Canonbury Square. In 1945, Eileen died suddenly and unexpectedly, during a hysterectomy operation. Orwell's own health was poor (he had been declared unfit for wartime service), but he worked constantly, producing countless articles, book reviews and columns, often for low fees, while a succession of housekeepers helped him look after Richard. His fortunes changed when the novel he rescued from the rubble in Kilburn was finally published. It was *Animal Farm*, his satirical take on Stalinism, and it was very successful. Although friends described his life and his flat at Canonbury Square as bleak, Orwell felt his work as an author was progressing, and that he had more good books to write.

Orwell wrote much of his last masterpiece, *Nineteen Eighty-Four*, at Canonbury Square and at a house on the island of Jura in the Inner Hebrides where he went for peace and quiet away from London. Both homes were basic, and even London could be bitterly cold, especially in the hard winter of 1946–47, when the cold was made worse because of the post-war fuel shortage. Orwell, who was already suffering from the lung problems that would kill him in a few years' time, wrote that he had to burn furniture, including an old bedstead, to keep warm.

Thanks to his last two novels, to non-fiction books such as *The Road to Wigan Pier*, and to his many essays, George Orwell is regarded as one of the greatest British writers of the 20th century. Although he lived in and wrote about many different places, from Burma to Spain, much of his work, from his study of the poor in *Down and Out in Paris and London* to *Nineteen Eighty-Four*, is rooted in the capital. His books, with their insistence on truthfulness, their disdain for totalitarianism, and their suspicion of everything from cults of personality to mass surveillance, still have a great deal to say to us today.

Jane Austen's House

CHAWTON, HAMPSHIRE

The novels of Jane Austen are read all over the world. Although they are set in a socially limited world – that of mainly middle-class people and landed gentry in the English countryside – their author's depiction of characters and social situations and her often wry humour have made her works universally popular. Characters such as Elizabeth Bennett and Mr Darcy, Emma and Mr Knightley, make a deep and lasting impression, and more and more people are engaged by them through the film adaptations of Austen's books. Most of her completed novels were written in the last eight years of her life, when she was living at Chawton, Hampshire, where her house is now preserved as a museum. Jane Austen's House Museum is a moving memorial not only to the writer herself, but also to the way of life she chronicled so precisely.

Jane Austen's father died in 1805 and the writer, her mother and sisters were left with little money. They moved to Chawton in 1809 because the novelist's brother, who owned the house, offered it to them rent free. Jane Austen lived there for her remaining eight years of life.

The house at Chawton – often known in Austen's time simply as 'the cottage' – was big enough for the family but modest architecturally. Its red-brick walls and tiled roof are typical of this part of southern England. It had been a farm house and, briefly, an inn, and was in an area that would have been familiar to the family as it was only about 15 miles away from their former home at Steventon. They lived a quiet life there, entertaining little apart from on family occasions, so there were relatively few distractions and Austen was able increasingly to concentrate on her writing.

Much of Jane Austen's work as a novelist was done at Chawton. Having already written *Sense and Sensibility* and *Pride and Prejudice*, she revised them for publication at Chawton. She also wrote *Mansfield Park*, *Emma* and *Persuasion* there. All this work was done discreetly, with the author tidying away her work when visitors came to call, because writing novels for money was not thought a proper occupation for a young woman from a respectable family in Georgian England. Austen's novels were originally published anonymously and only when *Northanger Abbey* and *Persuasion* came out after her death did a preface reveal the author's identity.

Jane Austen died young, of Addison's disease, in 1817. Her mother and sister continued to live at Chawton until they died, when the building was converted into accommodation for labourers. At the beginning of the 20th century the building's owner, Edward Knight, put it up for sale. The Jane Austen Society appealed for help to preserve the house and Thomas Edward Carpenter purchased it, allowing the museum to be established, and opened to the public in 1949. It contains early editions of Jane Austen's books, together with furniture and possessions from the family, and personal items owned by the novelist including three pieces of her jewellery and several music manuscripts that she copied out. Most evocative of all of her work as a writer are some of her letters and the table at which she often wrote. These objects combine with the unpretentious atmosphere of the house and its beautiful gardens to evoke the setting in which Jane Austen wrote her much-loved novels.

Abbey Road Studios

ST JOHN'S WOOD, LONDON

When the Beatles released their Abbey Road album in 1969, they made famous the address of the EMI studios where the disc was produced. The album cover showed a photograph by Iain Macmillan of the four members of the band on the zebra crossing in the quiet North London street where the recording sessions took place, and the studio, renamed Abbey Road Studios, acquired instant fame. Since then, people have been aware of the place where the Beatles, Pink Floyd, Buzzcocks and Blur recorded. But few realise that Abbey Road has a much longer musical history.

The studios in Abbey Road were first opened in 1931, when the Gramophone Company bought a 100-year-old town house and turned it into a venue for recording music. To make the building large enough, they built an extension on the back, and the studios were opened when the composer Edward Elgar conducted sessions of his own music with the London Symphony Orchestra. Elgar, who was 74 in 1931, had always been a keen advocate of recording, following the changing technology as it improved and making many recordings of his works. He was followed to Abbey Road by many other illustrious classical musicians.

From the early days, the engineers at Abbey Road were keen to use the latest technology to get the best sound. The Gramophone Company merged with Columbia Gramophone Company to create EMI shortly after the studio was founded, and one of their key employees was engineer Alan Blumlein, the inventor of modern stereo sound. Stereo recording at Abbey Road began in 1934, with a recording of Mozart's Symphony No 41, *Jupiter*. Digital recording was also pioneered there in the late 1970s, with a single by the jazz-fusion band Morrissey-Mullen. As one of the most prominent studios in the world, Abbey Road continues to use the latest and best in recording technology, with equipment capable of capturing everything from solo piano music to the most lavishly orchestrated film scores such as those for *Star Wars* or *Lord of the Rings*.

Since its opening with Elgar, Abbey Road has worked with musicians working in every style and genre. Fats Waller, Glenn Miller and Ella Fitzgerald recorded there; so did Noël Coward and Marlene Dietrich; so have Adele and Dido. Because of EMI's major role in classical music, the studios have also hosted musicians such as Yehudi Menuhin, Arthur Rubinstein and Plácido Domingo.

Iain Macmillan only had 15 minutes to take the now-famous photograph for the cover of the Beatles' Abbey Road album. But the image and album title made the general public aware, as never before, of the importance of the studios in the working lives of the band – and, by extension, of the thousands of other musicians who have recorded there. It also helped to publicise the important work done by the backroom people of the music business, the engineers and producers – people like the Beatles' celebrated producer George Martin – who did so much to enable musicians to create the sounds they wanted. Music is, by definition, a noisy business, and is often conducted in the glare of publicity. But it is appropriate that this vital but less understood and appreciated aspect of the art should have one of its foremost homes not in Soho or on Broadway but in a quiet residential street in a Georgian house in North London.

48 Doughty Street

LONDON

The 25-year-old novelist Charles Dickens and his young family moved into the Georgian townhouse at 48 Doughty Street in 1837. Dickens had many different addresses during his busy life, but Doughty Street is the only one of his houses that has been made into a museum about the writer. He had a three-year lease on the house, but in the event only lived there between March 1837 and December 1839, before he and his growing family moved to a larger house. However, those years were important ones for Dickens. He held down a job as editor of the literary magazine *Bentley's Miscellany*, while also producing a great deal of fiction and several plays. In his time at Doughty Street he finished his first two novels, *The Pickwick Papers* and *Oliver Twist*, and began to work on the next two, *Nicholas Nickleby* and *Barnaby Rudge*. These books, brought out initially in instalments, proved very popular and made Dickens famous. His time in Doughty Street marked the first turning point in his career.

Dickens and his wife Catherine moved to Doughty Street because their previous home, in Furnival's Inn, was too small for their growing family. Their first son Charley was born in January 1837 and two daughters arrived during their time in the house. They also shared the Doughty Street house with Dickens' brother Frederick and Catherine's sister Mary, together with a cook, a housemaid, a nurse, and a manservant. The house had room for all these people, as well as for a separate study for Charles, where he wrote his novels and the increasing number of newspaper and magazine articles that flowed from his pen.

The writer seems to have enjoyed having a sizeable house for the first time in his life. Richard Bentley, his boss at *Bentley's Miscellany*, loaned him money to cover moving expenses and Dickens furnished the house, choosing the delicate Regency and William IV period furniture that he preferred to the heavier pieces that were then coming into fashion. He installed the mirrors that he loved and painted the interior walls in bright colours – he chose pink woodwork for some rooms.

The family's first few weeks in Doughty Street were happy, but in May 1837 Catherine's sister Mary died suddenly, apparently of heart failure; she was only 17 years old. This loss affected Dickens very deeply. He adored Mary, seeing her as a young woman who combined beauty and virtue, and some critics believe that a number of young female characters in his novels – including Little Nell in *Nicholas Nickleby* and Florence Dombey in *Dombey and Son* – were based on her. This could, then, be another way in which his time in the house was formative for Dickens.

By the time he left Doughty Street for a still larger house, Dickens had already embraced some of his favourite social themes, such as child poverty and education, and had many enthusiastic readers who would follow him as he produced his string of later novels. His readership was growing rapidly: the first instalment of *Pickwick Papers* sold about 500 copies; the last sold more than 40,000.

In 1923, 48 Doughty Street was threatened with demolition. The Dickens Fellowship, an organisation of Dickens enthusiasts, bought the house and it was restored and made into a museum, now in the care of a separate trust. The house contains a collection of Dickens' manuscripts, letters, first editions and other materials, together with many of the novelist's possessions, including the desk at which he wrote his books. Rooms furnished as they would have been in Dickens' time show the kind of life lived by the family and their servants, taking one close to the domestic world of Britain's best known novelist, in the heart of the city that inspired so much of his writing.

The Haçienda

WHITWORTH STREET WEST, MANCHESTER

The Haçienda was a nightclub that presided over a transformation of the music scene in Manchester in the 1980s and 1990s, and heralded the new genres of house and rave music. The club was financed by Tony Wilson, the head of Factory Records, and the members of the band New Order and the band's manager, Rob Gretton. It was open between 1982 and 1997 in a former industrial building near the centre of Manchester. The red-brick Victorian building had been the showroom and warehouse of a yacht company, and had a striking curved façade on a street corner.

The club's interior was designed by Ben Kelly, who was recommended to the Factory team by Peter Saville, the designer of their record sleeves. Kelly created an interior with industrial metal roof trusses topped by glazing, looking down on a space with stripped-down decor made striking mainly by a great deal of yellow and black-striped security tape. Inside the team exercised their wit on naming the various rooms. The downstairs cocktail bar was called the Gay Traitor, an allusion to the art historian and spy Anthony Blunt; other bars were named Kim Philby and Hicks (the code name of Guy Burgess). The name of the club itself came from a line in a Situationist text by Ivan Chtcheglov, 'The hacienda must be built'.

What set the club apart, however, was the music played there. The Haçienda had the knack of attracting bands before they were well known. Frankie Goes To Hollywood and Culture Club played there in their early days and Madonna had her first UK gig at the Haçienda, as part of an edition of *The Tube* on Channel 4. Manchester bands who soon became nationally and internationally known played there – the club hosted The Smiths, The Fall, and, naturally, New Order, as well as musicians from elsewhere like Sheffieldians Cabaret Voltaire and the Thompson Twins. The club was known particularly for bands from the upcoming 'Madchester' scene, who were playing a blend of alternative rock, acid house, pyschedelia and other genres, again bringing Manchester's music into national focus. Just as influential were the club's DJ nights. The Haçienda became especially famous for house music, especially as played at the club's 'Hot' night, which was hosted by Mike Pickering and Jon DaSilva in 1988.

House music in the late 1980s was inseparable from the consumption of drugs, especially ecstasy, and the Haçienda had its share of drug-related issues. These came to a tragic head in July 1989, when the first ecstasy-related fatality in the UK took place at the club with the death of teenager Clare Leighton. There were also problems with violence inside the club and on the street and the Haçienda closed for a few months in 1991. After reopening, the venue continued until 1997, when the final closure occurred. Although some security problems had persisted, the main reason for closure was that the club was losing money.

After standing empty for some years, the building was eventually demolished in 2002 and a block of apartments was built on the site. The Haçienda name was retained for the development, and the new building has a curving brick frontage like that of the original, although its millennial modernist style is otherwise dissimilar. The name, however, like the best of the music, lives on.

100 Club

OXFORD STREET, LONDON

One day in 1942 a tailor called Robert Feldman stopped for a cup of tea in a basement restaurant in Oxford Street and decided the place would make an ideal music venue. Before the end of the year the restaurant was hosting the Robert Feldman Swing Club every Sunday. Fans of swing music, then the latest craze, turned up to hear musicians like tenor saxophonist Jimmy Skidmore, already well known for his work with musicians such as George Shearing, and younger players such as trumpeter Kenny Baker, who had just made his first record. Thanks to the likes of Glenn Miller, swing was popular in the USA, and soon many GIs were turning up and they were followed by American musicians such as Art Pepper and Benny Goodman. Glenn Miller himself came, both as a player and as a member of the audience. For jazz fans, especially those who liked to dance, the club proved to be a welcome distraction from the war. The venue even adopted a slogan with the words: 'Forget the doodlebug – come and jitterbug'.

Feldman's club was well established as a jazz venue by the post-war period. It changed hands, and names, twice. First, in the 1950s, it was owned by Lyn Dutton; he was agent to the popular band leader Humphrey Lyttelton, whose name replaced Feldman's above the door. Lyttelton's 1956 hit 'Bad Penny Blues' started a boom for Trad jazz, and the club became the place to go and hear it. In 1964, the place changed hands again, and this time was given its lasting name, the 100 Club, under new owner Roger Horton.

Horton widened the club's appeal in the 1960s and onwards. As well as traditional jazz, there was also blues (with appearances by artists of the calibre of B B King) and rhythm and blues (from Bo Diddley among others). In the 1970s the club became famous for Punk rock: the Sex Pistols, Siouxsie and the Banshees, Buzzcocks, The Clash and The Jam all played in Oxford Street. Jazz, soul and northern soul, also featured on different nights. There is also a history of unadvertised or 'secret' gigs by famous artists. Bands such as the Rolling Stones, not normally used to performing in a venue holding just 350 people, have played the 100 Club. And finally, on particular nights, the swing and traditional jazz that got the club off to its popular start still feature, acknowledging the club's history and pleasing fans.

This rich and varied musical history makes the 100 Club one of the greatest musical venues in the country, a place that has been a forum for the latest in new genres and styles, but also a venue to which established artists have returned. Few other small-scale venues can boast of having staged performances from musicians as diverse as Louis Armstrong and David Bowie, Bob Dylan and Glenn Miller, Jimi Hendrix and Paul McCartney. The setting might look unpromising – the decor has not changed much since the Punk era – but that is part of its character and part of what people like about it: it is the music that counts, and the music played at the 100 Club is testimony to Britain's unique openness to styles, ages and genres.

Handel and Hendrix in London

23 AND 25 BROOK STREET, LONDON

Numbers 23 and 25 Brook Street in Central London do not look very remarkable today. The buildings' ground floors are occupied by shops, while upstairs there are brick walls and sash windows typical of the early 18th-century development of this part of London. What is special about these houses is their former occupants: they were home to two of the most famous and influential musicians to live in London, in the 18th century George Frideric Handel and in the 20th century Jimi Hendrix.

Handel was born in Germany, but made his home in London from 1712 onwards. He moved to Brook Street in 1723 and lived there for the rest of his life, on a series of short leases. He must have liked the house because it was convenient for the King's Theatre, Haymarket, where many of his operas were staged, but far enough away from the bustle of more crowded London districts such as Soho or Covent Garden to give him some peace to compose. Handel was unmarried, and the house was a sizeable one for a single man, but the composer had servants, and wanted space to set aside rooms for composing and rehearsing – and, as a keyboard player, he needed space for his instruments, which included a harpsichord, an organ and a clavichord.

The London years were successful ones for Handel. He responded well to musical fashion, composing first Italian operas then later, when these fell out of favour with audiences, oratorios, choral works on Biblical themes. He also wrote a great deal of instrumental music, from concertos and chamber pieces to grand ceremonial music such as the Music for the Royal Fireworks, which attracted an audience of 12,000 when rehearsed in Vauxhall Gardens in 1749. Handel was a hugely popular composer, and his works are still often performed. Choral music became widely popular in England largely as a result of performances of Handel's oratorios, and these have remained a mainstay of choral societies all over the country.

By the late 20th century Brook Street had changed. Rather than a quiet, upper-middle-class residential street it was now part of the shopping district of London's West End – it is only a few minutes' walk south of Oxford Street. With shops occupying the ground floors, many houses were divided into flats upstairs. In 1968 the flat at 23 Brook Street was advertised and the person who responded to the advertisement was Kathy Etchingham, girlfriend of the American guitarist, singer and songwriter Jimi Hendrix. Hendrix moved in soon afterwards, furnishing the flat before going off on a US tour. He did not stay long in Brook Street, going back to New York in March 1969, but spoke of the flat as his first proper home.

Jimi Hendrix first came to London in 1966. The same year, he formed his band, The Jimi Hendrix Experience, with British musicians Noel Redding on bass and Mitch Mitchell on drums, and by May 1967 had had three top-ten hits in the UK, 'Hey Joe', 'Purple Haze', and 'The Wind Cries Mary'. Also in 1967 he played at the Monterey Pop Festival, which brought him fame in the US. In 1969 he headlined at Woodstock in the US, and back in the UK in 1970 he headlined at the Isle of Wight Festival.

If Handel changed the world of 18th-century music, Hendrix had a similar impact in the late 20th century. He won fame because his loud music and intense stage presence exemplified the way the guitar was seen as an instrument of rebellion. But his musical influence went much deeper than this. He extended the scope and sound palette of the electric guitar and brought a new kind of expressiveness to rock and blues. Also like Handel, Hendrix chose to live in Britain, and he did his most influential work with British musicians. Although he lived in Brook Street for a short time, his time in Britain was transformational.

6 Loss and Destruction

Crystal Palace

HYDE PARK AND SYDENHAM, LONDON

The Crystal Palace was one of the most remarkable buildings of the Victorian era. Conceived as an exhibition hall for the Great Exhibition of 1851, it and its contents amazed and entertained millions of people and its destruction in a fire was a major loss to the capital. It was also a hugely influential building in the history of architecture.

In 1849, the civil servant Henry Cole proposed a great international exhibition of the arts and industrial products of the world, to be held in 1851. With the backing of Prince Albert, a site was agreed in London's Hyde Park, and a competition to produce a design for a temporary exhibition hall attracted 227 entries. However, none of these proposals seemed suitable to the exhibition committee – most were too expensive, or would take too long to build. The committee therefore commissioned their own design, but it was so bad that the press, and virtually everyone else, ridiculed it. They were rescued by Jospeh Paxton, a gardener and garden designer who worked for the Duke of Devonshire.

Paxton used his knowledge of large-scale greenhouse construction to design the exhibition hall in glass and cast iron. The structure was immense – 1,848 feet long and 408 feet across. To build this enormous structure in the short time allowed, Paxton used modular construction, basing his design around the size of the largest panes of glass that it was then possible to make; 300,000 of these panes were needed for the vast building. This method of construction meant that all the components – columns, beams, gutters, glazing bars, and panes of glass – could be mass produced off-site to standard sizes and designs. They were then delivered to Hyde Park as the contractors assembled the building and this 'kit of parts' approach meant that assembly was amazingly fast. Building work started in July 1850 and the vast hall was ready (and on budget) before the exhibition's opening on 1 May 1851.

The building immediately impressed exhibitors, visitors and the press. Someone, probably the writer Douglas Jerrold, referred to it as a 'crystal palace', and the name stuck. Some six million visitors came to the exhibition between May and October 1851 to look at the 100,000 exhibits, half from the British empire, half from the rest of the world, and to marvel at the building. After the exhibition closed, the Crystal Palace, intended to be a temporary building, was taken apart and re-erected on Sydenham Hill, South London, as a venue for further exhibitions and concerts. The rebuilt Crystal Palace (pictured) was even larger and more magnificent than before. Paxton added a semi-circular barrel vault to the nave and incorporated two new transepts, to give even more space inside. Linked to Central London by train, the enlarged Crystal Palace continued to draw visitors.

The Crystal Palace remained a major London attraction until the night of 30 November 1936, when it caught fire. The blaze spread quickly, thanks to the building's many flammable contents, and the efforts of 400 firemen were not enough to stop it. The Crystal Palace was not adequately insured and could not be rebuilt. It is remembered as one of the greatest symbols of the Victorians' optimism, technological flair and empire-building. Anyone who visits the site today can see the foundations of the remarkable building. Its vast extent is as amazing now as it must have been 150 years ago.

Farfield Inn

NEEPSEND LANE, SHEFFIELD

The Farfield Inn, an 18th-century building in the Sheffield area of Neepsend, was caught up in one of the country's worst peacetime disasters, the Great Sheffield Flood of 1864. The flood occurred when the Dale Dyke Dam at Bradfield collapsed, letting loose about 700 million gallons of water, which surged downstream along the Loxley and Don rivers, inundating large parts of Sheffield. The flood killed at least 240 people and flattened some 600 houses. The Farfield Inn and its landlady Matilda Mason were lucky survivors.

Dale Dyke Dam and its accompanying reservoir were new structures, built to supply mills in the Loxley Valley and to provide running water to part of Sheffield. The builders, the Sheffield Waterworks Company, completed the project in March 1864 and on 11 March were filling the reservoir, when at about 5.30 in the afternoon a workman noticed a crack in the embankment. As the crack began to widen, the project's engineer, John Gunson, was called in. Gunson attempted to take remedial action but before midnight, the dam had burst, unleashing an overwhelming torrent. The reservoir took only 47 minutes to empty, by which time over 5,000 homes and workplaces were flooded. The official death toll of 240 may well have been higher; some modern historians put it at nearer 300.

One building somehow resisted the relentless power of the water. The Farfield Inn stood firm, and Matilda Mason took refuge on an upper floor as the water inundated the public rooms below. Her survival was a triumph, but her business was badly affected. Most of the locals who did not perish in the flood had to move out of the area. Matilda, like the other survivors of the disaster, was in desperate need. By October, a board of commissioners had been set up by the government to process claims for compensation. There were 7,000 claims, and Matilda Mason was among the claimants: she was awarded £162 13s 9d, an indication that there must have been considerable damage to the pub, its fittings and her stock.

What caused the disaster? Most people held the Sheffield Waterworks Company responsible, and the government's inspectors agreed. The inspectors pointed specifically to the company's engineers, John Gunson and John Leather. The jury at the inquest also blamed the engineers and the poor quality of the construction. However, a committee of civil engineers disagreed, reporting that the structure was sound, and would have held had there not been a movement in the ground beneath the dam.

Even if, as the engineers believed, the dam was built properly according to the standards of the time, there were clearly aspects that needed to be improved and the government inspectors cited the way the embankment had been constructed, the position of the outlet pipes, and the thickness of the puddle wall as concerns to be addressed when the dam was rebuilt – this time, prudently, at a smaller scale.

The Great Sheffield Flood was not only one of Britain's worst peacetime disasters, it was also one of the first to be covered by mass media. Newspapers reported it widely, and highlighted not only the loss of life and property, but also the question of corporate responsibility. By giving this issue the publicity it deserved, the press helped to hasten the coming of tighter regulation for water companies, and for public projects generally. The Farfield Inn remains as a reminder of the disaster, and of the personal tragedies and traumas that it brought.

The Euston Arch

EUSTON STATION, LONDON

London's Euston Station was opened in 1837 as the capital's gateway to the Midlands and northern England. Its owners, the London and Birmingham Railway, signposted their terminus by building a gigantic gateway flanked by lodges to signal its presence. This gateway, designed by the railway's architect Philip Hardwick in the then-fashionable Greek revival style, was in the form of a Doric portico, Doric being the plainest of the three ancient Greek orders and the one used on the Parthenon in Athens. At 70 feet high and with columns more than 8 feet in diameter, it towered above those entering the station, even if they did so by carriage. It was instantly recognisable, and soon became known as the Euston Arch.

The Euston Arch led into a courtyard to one side the station. It had no practical purpose, but had a major symbolic role. It made the station easy to recognise and locate from a distance, and its size and Classical design stood both for the prominence of the railway company and the importance of the terminus. It was as if passengers were about to set off along a ceremonial route – all the way to Birmingham, or beyond. The great sandstone gateway – it was not, strictly, an arch at all – became a nationally known symbol of the railway.

With its massive columns and solid stone walls, the Euston Arch looked indestructible. It survived a plan to redevelop the station and demolish it in 1938, and it came through the bombardment of World War II. But by the early 1960s there was a pressing need to modernise Euston Station by enlarging it and making it ready for the electrification of the line between Euston and Scotland. By this time the arch was a listed building, so getting permission to demolish it was not straightforward.

Many people opposed demolition. The journalist Woodrow Wyatt, the poet John Betjeman and the architectural historian Nikolaus Pevsner all campaigned for its preservation. So did J M Richards, editor of the *Architectural Review*. Richards was usually an enthusiast for modern architecture, but recognised the importance of the arch. The Society for the Protection of Ancient Buildings, the Georgian Group, and the London Society all lobbied to keep the arch. The Victorian Society did so too: they asked for a delay so that Betjeman, the Society's vice-chairman, could start a fund-raising campaign to get together the money needed to take the building apart and relocate it.

None of these efforts was successful, and work on the demolition of the arch was begun in December 1961. It was a painstaking process, involving taking the arch apart by hand, because of the danger posed by explosives. Frank Valori, head of the demolition company, Leonard Fairclough, offered to store the stone at his own expense until a new site for the arch could be found. This offer was rejected by the authorities, and much of the masonry was used as infill in the Prescott Channel, which feeds into the River Lea in Northeast London.

The Euston Arch was an important monument to the development of the railways in Britain, and a notable symbol of the railway network that linked London with the Midlands and the North. It was also a major – and much loved – part of the cityscape of this part of London. However, still more important were the implications of the demolition for the future of architectural preservation. It had perished in spite of a campaign led by several respected, high-profile individuals. Conservationists realised that they had to be highly organised if they wanted to prevent the demolition of important buildings – especially 19th-century buildings, which were then highly unfashionable. The loss of the Euston Arch was a wake-up call.

The Monument

MONUMENT STREET AND FISH STREET HILL, LONDON

The tall column known simply as the Monument marks one of the greatest moments of loss and destruction this country has known: the 1666 Great Fire of London. The fire began at the premises of a baker, Thomas Farriner, in Pudding Lane, soon after midnight on 2 September 1666. It took hold and spread through London's buildings, many of which were timber-framed, with thatched roofs. Flammable trade goods – such as tallow, oil, pitch, coal, turpentine and gunpowder – stored in riverside warehouses also fed the fire. The flames were fanned by the wind and the fire burned for three days, destroying most of the City of London between the Tower and Temple Bar, which was then the city's western gateway. St Paul's Cathedral, 87 churches, some 40 livery halls, city prisons, and around 13,000 houses were destroyed. There were officially only a handful of deaths, but the real casualties – those who went unrecorded, and those who perished later trying to survive in hastily erected temporary camps – must have been much greater. The job of rebuilding took years. In the process, London acquired some of its finest buildings, especially 51 new churches and St Paul's Cathedral, designed by Wren.

King Charles II was keen that there should be a monument to mark the tragedy of the fire and to commemorate the reconstruction. The first Rebuilding Act provided for a column of brass or stone, on or near the site of the bakery where the fire started, 'the better to preserve the memory of this dreadful visitation'. Various designs – including an obelisk and a pillar covered with 'tongues of fire' – were proposed, and eventually a Doric column was chosen. In 1671, Wren produced a wooden model of a suitable design, and this was approved by the City authorities. Although the architect was probably working with his friend Robert Hooke, who produced some of the drawings for alternative designs for the column, the overall design is usually attributed to Wren.

The Monument is 202 feet tall, this also being the distance from the site to Farriner's bakery. Building it was a major task, in part because the design provided for a spiral staircase leading to a viewing platform at the top. Construction did not begin straight away – there were still many pressing demands on building stone and builders' time – but by 1675, the column was nearly complete.

Wren's initial idea was to top the column with a statue of King Charles II; then he decided on a sculpture of a phoenix, to symbolise the rebirth of London after the fire. But as the column rose, he changed his mind: he was concerned that the bird's outstretched wings would act like sails in the wind and bring the sculpture tumbling down. In the end a flaming urn in gilt-bronze was chosen to sit at the top of the column. Inscriptions at the base commemorated the fire and reported that London was rebuilt in three years – which was nowhere near true. The carved relief on the pedestal is the work of Caius Gabriel Cibber. It shows a female figure representing London, being supported by another figure, Time. Charles II and his brother the Duke of York (the future James II) look on and the king commands his followers to help the city. Allegorical figures representing Science, Architecture and Liberty add their support.

In spite of its inscription, exaggerating the speed at which the city was rebuilt, and the fanciful, but beautifully carved relief, the Monument is an enduring reminder of the losses of the Great Fire and of the turning point in its history that produced so many buildings, such as St Paul's and the surviving city churches, that still adorn London.

Greyfriars Monastery and the village of Dunwich

SUFFOLK

Dunwich on the coast of Suffolk is now a small village but in the Middle Ages it was a sizeable town and a sea port. By the 13th century it had several churches and had expanded into a major centre of sea trade, fishing and ship building. In this period the town covered an area similar to the city of London and may have had a population of around 5,000, together with five monastic houses (including two friaries), and probably a mint and a guildhall.

However, in the late 13th and early 14th centuries, major storms destroyed the prosperity of Dunwich. The storms began in 1286 and 1287. The rough seas shifted large amounts of coastal gravel, extending a spit and blocking the harbour. Over time, the coastline itself steadily eroded away. There were further major storms in 1328, 1347 and 1362. Their combined effect was a steep decline in the sea trade followed by the complete disappearance of the strip of land that contained most of the town. Numerous churches, the guildhall and hundreds of houses all vanished, and the relentless process of coastal erosion continued for hundreds of years. By the mid-16th century, even the marketplace had gone, and a map of 1587 shows that half of the medieval town had disappeared into the sea. Dunwich was no longer a town in anything but name. The last of the medieval churches, All Saints', succumbed to the sea in the early 20th century: its tower, the last part to remain standing, slipped into the water in November 1919.

Medieval Dunwich was home to two communities of friars. The friary of the Dominicans, or Black Friars, survived until Henry VIII closed it in the 16th century but its buildings were lost to the sea in 1717. Dunwich's other group of friars were Franciscans, or Grey Friars. Their friary and church were a little further inland so they too survived until the Dissolution. The friary was founded in the mid-13th century and in 1277 there were 20 friars based there. Friars were usually based in towns, because they were concerned with preaching to the lay population rather than secluding themselves from the secular world like the other monastic orders. They moved to the current friary site in 1290, when Edward I granted them land on what was then the western side of the town and they seem to have been successful because their friary site was extended to the south, probably at the end of the 14th or beginning of the 15th century.

Greyfriars continued until dissolved by Henry VIII in 1538, when the buildings were converted into a large house, shown on the 1587 map of the town. However, most of the additions were later demolished and what survive now are ruins of some of the friars' buildings – including the refectory, entrance gateway and part of the surrounding precinct wall. The foundations of the friars' church, infirmary and other buildings survive as buried remains. Although fragmentary, the ruins of the friary are very valuable because so many medieval friaries have vanished completely beneath later buildings and roads in England's crowded towns. They are also a salutary reminder of Dunwich's decline: originally towards the western side of the town, the ruins are now very near the sea that swallowed the once-large settlement that disappeared thanks to a process of coastal erosion and change that continues to this day.

The *Mary Rose*

Henry VIII's flagship the *Mary Rose* took part in three campaigns against France in the early 16th century but was sunk during the Battle of the Solent on 19 July 1545. In 1982 in a major marine archaeological project, the wreck of the ship was raised and many of the items on board were brought to the surface and preserved. The finds have given historians unique insights, not only into the history of the English navy, but also into countless other aspects of 16th-century life, from the history of surgery to the development of musical instruments, from Tudor costume to the techniques of navigation.

It is not known exactly why the *Mary Rose* sank. According to contemporary accounts, she keeled over to one side while making a turn, and when this happened water flowed into unclosed cannon openings. This suggests that the ship was unstable, perhaps because she was overloaded or because of modifications made to her structure during a recent refit. Historians knew from early accounts roughly where she lay, and divers found the vessel in 1836, but lost the wreck again. Her precise location was not confirmed until 1971.

Once they had located the remains of the *Mary Rose*, archaeologists began to recover thousands of artefacts, together with the remains of many of the crew. The interest of the objects was immediately obvious. In the cabin of the ship's master carpenter, for example, were not only his tools but also a chest containing his personal belongings – from useful items like plates and a tankard to luxuries such as a sundial and a backgammon set, quite high-status possessions that suggest a man who was well paid. Perhaps the carpenter also had a pet dog – a dog's skeleton was found just outside his cabin. A chest belonging to the ship's barber-surgeon also revealed items of some sophistication, such as a metal syringe, a wooden feeding bottle, and numerous containers of medicine made from herbal ingredients.

Among the thousands of other finds are musical instruments (including a very early fiddle and a unique type of shawm, the ancestor of the modern oboe), fine-toothed combs for removing nits from hair, numerous leather shoes preserved in the water (leather goods from this period are otherwise rare), and even clothes such as a woollen jerkin. Finds of weaponry, from cannon to longbows, have increased historians' knowledge of Tudor warfare. And the skeletons of the sailors themselves have yielded all kinds of information about their life and health, including many mended fractures, as one would expect to find in the bones of experienced fighting men.

The remains of the ship itself were equally revealing. The *Mary Rose* was one of the earliest purpose-built English warships, and a fascinating structure, in the form of a carrack (a ship with a high 'castle' structure at each end), with dozens of openings for firing cannon. A large part of half of the hull still lay on the sea bed, protected by the mud. A long and complex operation to raise it came to a climax in October 1982, when the ship was brought to the surface. Since then, the hull has been carefully conserved, comprehensively studied, and is now on display along with many of the artefacts in the purpose-built Mary Rose Museum. The whole project was a revelation, stretching the techniques of marine archaeology, revealing an unprecedented amount about life in the Tudor period, and making much of this information accessible to the public.

Hillsborough Football Stadium

SHEFFIELD

The worst disaster in British sporting history occurred at the Hillsborough Stadium of Sheffield Wednesday Football Club during an F A Cup semi-final game between Liverpool and Nottingham Forest on 15 April 1989. The disaster began just before kick-off when, to avoid overcrowding at the entrance turnstiles, the senior police officer at the stadium, Chief Superintendent David Duckenfield, ordered exit gate C to be opened. This sent many Liverpool supporters into overcrowded standing-only pens in the stadium's Leppings Lane stand, forcing them into an unbearable and deadly crush. Many could not move as they were forced against the perimeter fencing, which was designed to prevent pitch invasions. Ninety-six people were killed, and hundreds more injured. Many of those who died did so from asphyxiation, because they were crushed so tightly together they simply could not breathe. Some found a route to safety by climbing over the perimeter fence on to the track surrounding the pitch, although the crush prevented many from doing this. Others were hauled to safety by spectators in the stand above. But many had no chance of escape.

Initially, David Duckenfield and his colleagues denied responsibility for the tragedy, saying that Liverpool fans had forced the exit gate open themselves. The attempts at a cover-up were compounded by some parts of the press, which falsely accused the Liverpool supporters of being drunk, or of engaging in hooliganism. There were also allegations – eventually shown to be untrue – that fans trying to get in without tickets, or with forged tickets, contributed to the crush. Many of these stories derived from the efforts of the police to shift blame on to the fans, something that continued in the weeks and months after the match and which had the effect of also covering up the inadequacy of their response once it was clear that a disaster was unfolding. The poor initial response of the ambulance service was also overlooked.

The first inquiry into the events at Hillsborough was overseen by Lord Justice Taylor. It reported in 1990, and concluded that the fans were not to blame and that things such as forged tickets were not factors in the disaster. Blame lay with the police who failed adequately to control the situation. When gate C was opened, leading supporters towards pens 3 and 4, these pens were already over-full. The report also came up with a number of conclusions about safety at football grounds, most notably recommending that stadia should be all-seater and that perimeter fences should be removed. However, the Director of Public Prosecutions ruled after the report that there was not sufficient evidence to prosecute individuals or institutions. The following year an inquest ruled that the deaths at Hillsborough were accidental.

The coroner's ruling and the refusal to prosecute anyone incensed the relatives of the victims and they campaigned long and hard for justice. Private prosecutions of David Duckenfield and his deputy failed and there was a legal ruling that a further inquiry was not justified. However, there was an independent review of the evidence, begun in 2009 and reporting in 2012, that revealed more evidence about the cover-ups and triggered a new inquest in 2014–2016. This produced verdicts of unlawful killing due to the failure of the police and ambulance services to fulfil their duty of care. The coroner rejected claims that the supporters were to blame for the disaster. Ultimately, six people were charged with offences including manslaughter by gross negligence and perverting the course of justice.

The families of the Hillsborough victims had to campaign for 25 years to get an inquest that considered the evidence and brought verdicts of unlawful killing. Their tenacity, in the face of denials, cover-ups and failures of the justice system, is remembered whenever the name Hillsborough is mentioned.

Must Farm
Bronze Age Settlement

WHITTLESEY, NEAR PETERBOROUGH

Discovered in 1999, the settlement at Must Farm, on the edge of a quarry near Peterborough, was soon revealed to be one of the most remarkable Bronze Age sites in Europe. Its preservation is due to unique circumstances: built over water, there was a disastrous fire when the houses were still new but fully occupied, and the buildings were quickly abandoned. The burning houses collapsed into the water, which extinguished the flames, leaving the remaining parts of the structures, plus the contents, to be preserved in the waterlogged ground beneath layers of protective silt. These objects give archaeologists a vivid insight into life in Bronze Age Britain in around 1000 BC.

The Must Farm settlement came to light when an archaeologist saw a series of wooden posts sticking out of the ground. Digs revealed that the houses were built over the river and supported on wooden poles. Some of the wattle – basket-work material – that made up the walls and floors of the buildings has survived. A protective palisade, also supported on wooden posts, was built around the whole settlement.

The collection of artefacts found among the remains of the settlement is remarkable. There are a number of bronze items, including axes of various different designs, swords, sickles, razors and a pair of shears. A lot of the metal tools, especially the axes, seem to have been very well used. It is probable that many of them were used to chop and work the hundreds of pieces of timber used in constructing the houses and palisade.

Archaeologists have unearthed a large number of pots, in a range of sizes and types from large storage jars to small cups. Pottery from the Bronze Age is not uncommon, but to find it still in the place where it was used is very unusual. Some of the vessels were even found as if they had been abandoned while in use, such as a bowl containing part of a meal, suggesting that its owner had stopped eating when the fire was discovered and someone raised the alarm.

Many wooden objects were preserved in the damp anaerobic conditions. Two wooden wheels, probably part of a horse-drawn cart, give insight into the people's technology and transport. A beautifully made and specially shaped box contained the metal shears. A metal axe was unearthed with part of its wooden haft still intact – a very rare find. Most fragile of all are the textile finds, pieces of finely woven cloth and even a ball of thread, showing the kinds of plant-based fibres that were used for clothing.

There is still work to be done on the finds. Some of the most exciting will be the analysis of traces of food found in the bottoms of many of the vessels. Further analysis of timber will probably yield more information about how the inhabitants used wood. Must Farm has already given archaeologists a greater range and depth of information about life 3,000 years ago than any other site. The continuing work on the finds will give yet further information, making Must Farm one of the most significant places for understanding our prehistoric past.

The wreck of the SS *Mendi*

OFF ST CATHERINE'S POINT, ISLE OF WIGHT

In January to February 1917, the SS *Mendi* was carrying 802 men of the South African Native Labour Corps from Cape Town to Plymouth and Le Havre. The Labour Corps was formed to provide vital support to the troops in World War I. It was not a fighting force but built railways, constructed roads, put up camps and dug trenches. The black South Africans who joined it did so with high hopes; many of those on board believed that by joining the Corps and helping the war effort, they would enhance the status of black people in South Africa and give them more political strength. But having travelled around 7,000 nautical miles from Africa, their troop ship was involved in a collision and 646 of those on board died, many perishing almost instantly in the ice-cold water.

In the early hours of the morning of 21 February 1917, there was thick fog in the Channel. Suddenly at 5 am, the *Darro*, a cargo ship of the Royal Mail Steam Packet Company collided with the *Mendi*. There was no warning – those on board the *Mendi* heard no fog horn – and the *Darro* was travelling at speed, so the impact was violent and the *Mendi* began to sink immediately. An unconfirmed account of the voyage relates how the pastor on board, Revd Isaac Dyobha, prepared the men for death immediately after the collision. He is said to have told them, 'Be quiet and calm, my countrymen, for what is taking place now is exactly what you came to do. You are going to die, but that is what you came to do.'

The blame for the tragedy fell squarely on the shoulders of Captain Stump of the *Darro*, who failed to sound his foghorn and was almost certainly travelling too fast. After the collision he sailed away without offering any help, and it was left to other vessels in the area, principally the destroyer HMS *Brisk*, to pick up the survivors. There were always question marks over the actions of Captain Stump. He was unable to explain adequately why he did not stop and help the victims. He said that it was dark and he could not see what was happening, but this was no reason not to stop and try to find out whether there were people in need of assistance. Survivors said that those on the *Darro* would have been able to hear their cries for help.

When the news of the tragedy reached South Africa, the dead men were praised by the Prime Minister, General Louis Botha, for their loyalty, but they received little other recognition. Although their deaths brought them some credit among South Africa's white rulers, this did not translate into political power and some members of the ANC had no words of praise for the Corps members because they felt that they had sold out to colonial government. For many years, the tragedy was not much reported or discussed by historians.

In recent decades, the tragedy has become more well known. In 1974, a British diver located the site of the wreck and established that the ship lay upright on the sea bed, but was beginning to break up. More recently, a desk-based assessment of the wreck was carried out, as a basis for further research. Memorials to those lost on board the *Mendi* have been erected in South Africa, France and the Netherlands, and at Southampton the names of those on the *Mendi* who have no known graves were added to the Hollybrook Memorial, which commemorates members of Commonwealth forces who were lost at sea. In South Africa itself, there is now a Mendi Medal, which is awarded to those who have shown exceptional bravery.

Whitby Abbey

NORTH YORKSHIRE

The monastery at Whitby is one of the oldest Christian sites in England, and was the scene of a turning point in the history of the early English church. During the post-Roman period Britain was divided into a number of separate kingdoms, and one of the most powerful of these was the Anglian kingdom of Northumbria (an area that included most of what are now Northumberland and Yorkshire). Edwin, king of Northumbria, was converted to Christianity in 627, and in about 657 the first monastery at Whitby was founded by a remarkable woman, Hild (or Hilda), Edwin's great-niece.

Hild's foundation was a double monastery, housing both monks and nuns, as was common in Anglo-Saxon England. Hild was highly respected – it was said that she was adviser to several kings – and her monastery produced some remarkable monks – five of Hild's monks became bishops and one was a remarkable writer, Caedmon, the first English poet whose name we know. In addition, Whitby hosted the important synod of 664, at which the Northumbrian king Oswiu chose the Roman strain of Christianity over the Celtic form of the faith, setting the direction of the English church for almost 900 years, until Henry VIII broke with Rome in the 16th century.

However, by the 9th century, the monastery founded by Hild seems to have been abandoned. The reason is not known for sure, but the likelihood is that attacks by Vikings were to blame for this first destruction of Whitby Abbey. Today there is no trace above ground of Hild's church or monastic buildings. After the Norman conquest of England, however, a new monastery was set up on the headland above Whitby. This was founded by the monk Reinfrid in 1078, and by 1100 it had an impressive church and monastic buildings, while a separate church for the local people was built nearby. From around 1225 onwards there was a major rebuilding, with much of the church reconstructed in the Gothic style. It is the high walls and pointed lancet windows of this building that are still visible, making one of the most beautiful and strikingly sited monastic ruins in the country.

This was a very large church and an ambitious architectural project. The choir, transepts, tower and part of the nave were finished before building work stopped – probably because money ran out – and the nave was completed later, in the 14th and 15th centuries. The building would have towered over the headland, looking down on the town below. But in 1539 the abbey closed as a result of Henry VIII's dissolution of the monasteries and the buildings were sold to Sir Richard Cholmley, a powerful Yorkshire landowner: Whitby's second phase of destruction was about to begin.

Although they made the abbey's domestic buildings into a house, the Cholmleys were not interested in the church and it gradually grew dilapidated. On its exposed site the building took a battering from wind and rain and through the 18th and 19th centuries the nave, tower and part of the transept and choir fell down, leaving the Romantic ruin visible today. By the end of the Victorian period, Whitby was a tourist town, well liked for its seaside location and well known as the setting of Bram Stoker's novel *Dracula*. Today, the abbey is still much visited for its role in the early history of British Christianity and for the beauty of its medieval Gothic buildings, their appearance made unforgettable by their ruined condition and their striking site on Whitby's headland.

7 Faith and Belief

Lindisfarne Priory

HOLY ISLAND, BERWICK-UPON-TWEED

Lindisfarne became an important centre of early Christianity in England in 635, when Oswald, king of Northumbria, invited the Irish monk Aidan to be bishop. Aidan travelled from his monastery in Iona to Lindisfarne, off the coast of Northeast England and a few miles from Oswald's palace at Bambrugh. Here Aidan and a group of other monks founded a monastery. He was based at Lindisfarne, but travelled widely in Northumbria, converting people to Christianity and founding churches. With the backing of Oswald, he was able to convert much of northern England to Christianity.

As a hub of northern Christianity, Lindisfarne became home to a number of notable scholars and evangelists. One of the most famous was Cuthbert, who came to Lindisfarne in the 670s and was appointed bishop in 685. After only two years in this role, he died and was buried in the church at Lindisfarne. When his tomb was opened, 11 years after his death, the monks found that his body had not decayed; this was deemed to be a miracle, and Cuthbert was venerated as a saint. Pilgrims were soon visiting Lindisfarne, and the monastery became wealthy, because kings and nobles granted it lands and other pilgrims brought gifts to Cuthbert's shrine. The monastery also became a major centre of scholarship, and its monks produced one of the greatest books of the period, the elaborately illuminated Lindisfarne Gospels. Now in the British Library, this book is stunningly adorned with the symbols of the Evangelists and richly coloured and gilded decorations featuring interlace patterns and images of birds and beasts; it is one of the artistic masterpieces of the period.

However, in 793 the first major Viking raid hit Britain, and Lindisfarne was its target. The monastery was damaged and desecrated and the monks retreated inland with their most precious relics. They spent some years as an itinerant community, leaving Lindisfarne permanently in 875 and building a new monastery at Chester-le-Street. Eventually St Cuthbert's remains found a permanent home in Durham. But Lindisfarne did not die as a Christian community. Various carved stones from the 9th and 10th centuries show that the Christian burial ground was still in use through this unsettled period.

At some time after the Norman conquest of England, the monastery at Lindisfarne was revived. A group of monks from Durham came to the site and, with the backing of the Scottish kings, built a new church and domestic buildings. Remains of these buildings still stand on the site today. Their exact date is not known, but there are records of a monk from Durham in Lindisfarne in 1122 and of a full-scale monastic community 50 years after that. It was always a small group and an outpost of Durham, but because Lindisfarne was Cuthbert's home and the site of his miracles, the place was revered and pilgrims still visited it. To set up even a small monastery there was a coup for the monks of Durham, because it meant that they maintained links with both sites associated with this important saint.

Lindisfarne's troubles returned at the end of the 13th century, when Edward I invaded Scotland and the borders became insecure. However, the monks fortified the priory and survived, maintaining their community until 1537, when Henry VIII began to dissolve the monasteries. The buildings were falling into ruin by the 18th century, when they became popular with visitors. If the 18th-century visitors were mainly interested in the picturesque views provided by the ruins, visitors today appreciate not only the beauty of the place but also the major role it played in the history of Christianity in England, and the amazing artistic legacy of the Lindisfarne Gospels.

Canterbury Cathedral and St Martin's Church

CANTERBURY, KENT

For some 1,600 years the dominant religion in Britain has been Christianity. The Christian religion has been hugely influential on every aspect of life on these islands, including not just ethics but also education, politics and art. The process of converting southern England to the faith began in Canterbury at the end of the 6th century, with the dynamic monk Augustine.

Christianity had come to England under the Romans, but when they left in the early 5th century, Britain was invaded by pagan Angles and Saxons. By the late 6th century, there were few Christians in England apart from in the west and in 597, Pope Gregory the Great decided to send the monk Augustine to England to convert the Anglo-Saxons. Augustine travelled to Kent, probably because its powerful king Aethelberht, himself a pagan, had a Christian wife, the Frankish princess Bertha, who was likely to welcome him. Although Aetlhelberht did not convert to Christianity immediately, he granted Augustine some land outside Canterbury's city walls, next to an old Roman church dedicated to St Martin.

The church of St Martin had fallen into disrepair after the Romans left, but Aethelberht restored it in about 580, for Bertha to use. It was Augustine's first base in England and when the king converted to Christianity a few years later he was baptised there. St Martin's survives and although it has been altered since the Saxon period – for example with the addition of a late-medieval tower – it remains the country's oldest parish church. Augustine built a monastery on the land near St Martin's and the support of the king and queen enabled it to prosper. Augustine built a further church, St Mary's, on the site and later, in the mid-8th century, yet another church, dedicated to St Pancras, was constructed. Augustine's foundation had become a major centre of Christian learning, to which many monks were drawn. But Augustine's influence extended far beyond the abbey walls – he was appointed the first archbishop of Canterbury, based at a church inside the city walls that became Canterbury Cathedral. Missionaries went out from Canterbury into the neighbouring Anglo-Saxon kingdoms, converting some of their rulers and beginning the steady spread of Christianity across southern England.

The abbey founded by Augustine continued to thrive in the centuries after his death. In the late 10th century it was led by Dunstan, another influential abbot, who imposed the new rule drawn up by St Benedict. Dunstan, who like Augustine became Archbishop of Canterbury, realised the importance of his predecessor's legacy, and changed the dedication of his church to include the name of its founder – it has been known as St Augustine's Abbey ever since.

Canterbury Cathedral, enlarged in the Anglo-Saxon period and rebuilt during the Middle Ages, became the most important church in England. With its three tall towers, it now dwarfs the ancient St Martin's and the ruined abbey of St Augustine. The cathedral has undergone several reconstructions and extensions, including a major rebuild after a fire in the 12th century, enlargement to include the shrine of the martyred Archbishop Thomas Beckett in the late 12th to 13th centuries, and the rebuilding of the nave in the 14th to 15th centuries. Thanks to these successive construction campaigns, Canterbury Cathedral is one of the country's greatest buildings, with outstanding architecture from the Romanesque crypt to the later medieval Gothic nave. As the seat of the country's senior Archbishop it is one of the most important religious centres in Britain.

Fountains Abbey

RIPON, NORTH YORKSHIRE

The remains of Fountains Abbey are among the most beautiful monastic ruins in Britain. They are an outstanding example of the architecture of the Cistercian order and a reminder of the huge change that came about in the 16th century, when Henry VIII dissolved England's monasteries.

The history of Fountains Abbey began in 1132, when 13 monks were expelled from the abbey of St Mary in York after a dispute. The rebel monks wanted to reform the regime at St Mary's because they thought it was too lax. They preferred the stricter rule of the Cistercian order and the Archbishop of York gave them land in the Skell valley in Yorkshire, so that they could start their own monastery.

The monks began to construct a small church in stone and a number of other buildings in wood. Their life in this isolated spot was hard for the first few years, but in 1135 they were joined by Hugh, who had been Dean of York. Hugh brought money to the new monastery and helped attract further benefactors, and the monks began to erect more permanent buildings. Construction work continued through the 13th century, by the end of which the monks had a substantial church and a very large complex of buildings in which to work, study, eat and sleep.

In spite of the fact that monks built up a substantial income from sheep farming and other enterprises, none of this was achieved without hardship – the abbey was attacked in the 12th century during a violent church dispute, was beset by economic troubles in the late 13th century, and then hit by Scottish raids in the 14th. Its fortunes were reflected in the number of monks in residence: by *c* 1300 there were around 50 monks and 200 lay brothers; in 1380 there were 34 monks and only 10 lay brothers. However, there was a resurgence after 1475, after which work was done to repair the buildings and construct the great tower.

It was a prosperous abbey that surrendered to Henry VIII in 1539 when he dissolved Fountains. The king's commissioners removed plate and vestments to the value of £700 and took control of 1,976 cattle, 1,146 sheep, 86 horses and 79 pigs. The king sold the abbey itself to Sir Richard Gresham, who removed the useful lead, glass, woodwork and furniture. Later the abbey was bought by Sir Stephen Proctor, who built Fountains Hall using stone from the infirmary and other abbey buildings. In 1768 the property passed to yet another family, the Aislabies, who added the abbey and its lands to their estate of Studley Royal. They turned the woods and valleys near Fountains into lavish water gardens with follies and statues and the ruins became a backdrop to these pleasure grounds – Fountains Abbey had in effect become the most impressive garden ornament in the country.

The walls of the church still stand almost to roof level and Abbot Huby's late-medieval tower still rises to its full height of 170 feet. There are also substantial remains of the buildings around the cloister, including the wing containing the kitchen and lay brothers' accommodation, the frater (dining room) and the chapter house. Many other buildings survive as low walls or foundations, showing the great extent of the complex site and the way the monastery was integrated with the River Skell, which provided both a clean water supply and drainage. The ruins of Fountains Abbey are thus hugely valuable for what they tell us about the lives of medieval Cistercian monks, who spent much of their time in prayer and study, and of the lay brothers who did most of the manual work on the abbey's farms. The remains are also a testimony to the huge loss that occurred at the Dissolution – and to the reuse by the place's later owners of the site, the abbey's stone, and the stunning ruins.

Farfield Meeting House

NEAR ADDINGHAM, WEST YORKSHIRE

The Religious Society of Friends, known popularly as the Quakers, began in the mid-17th century in Lancashire. They believed that God spoke directly to people through Christ, so they had no priests, liturgy or sacraments; other key beliefs and practices included opposing warfare and refusing to swear oaths. These beliefs set them apart from the Church of England, and meant that they (along with groups such as Presbyterians, Independents and Baptists) were categorised as nonconformists. These groups were frequently persecuted until in 1689 the Act of Toleration allowed them to worship freely, under certain conditions.

From 1689, Quakers began to build their own meeting houses, where they could worship in their own way. One of the very first was the Farfield Meeting House near Addingham in West Yorkshire. There had been Quakers in the area since the 1650s, when Anthony Myers, of Farfield Hall, met a group of Quakers and allowed them to worship at his home. In 1666 he gave them a 5,000-year lease on a plot of land where they could bury their dead, and in 1689 they built a meeting house adjoining the burial ground.

Like most early meeting houses, the one at Farfield is very simple architecturally – the Quakers in general shunned ostentation and, like other nonconformists, eschewed statues or other images in their places of worship. The meeting house is a rectangular building of rubble masonry with stone mullioned windows. Its grey stone walls and simple architecture fit perfectly into the surroundings – it could almost be a small cottage. Nearby are five table tombs of members of the Myers family. Although plain, these tombs are unusually large and ostentatious for Quaker graves – large tombs were more common among early Quakers, but many of these were removed after 1717, when the Quakers' Yearly Meeting condemned such memorials as a 'vain custom'. Most Quakers had very small stones or unmarked graves. The meeting house interior is also very simple, with plain white walls, wooden benches to sit on, and a raised dais or stand at one end where the group's elders sat.

Farfield Meeting House is an early example, but soon Quaker meeting houses were being built all over England, and members of the Society of Friends were increasingly respected for their integrity. Because nonconformists were not allowed to attend university, many Quakers went into business. Some of the country's most successful businesses, such as Fry's and Rowntree's, were run by Quakers, and members of these families also championed social reform and had a beneficial influence on wider society. These developments had their roots in the early Quaker communities based at meeting houses such as Farfield.

The meeting house remained in use by the Quakers until the 1890s. Subsequent uses included conversion to an artist's studio, which involved little alteration to the building. In 1994 the meeting house was transferred to the care of the Historic Chapels Trust, which repaired it and now looks after it. The Farfield Meeting House is preserved as one of the earliest purpose-built places of Quaker worship, and as a symbol of the importance of religious nonconformity in the history and culture of England in the 17th and subsequent centuries.

Brick Lane Jamme Masjid
SPITALFIELDS, LONDON

England's major cities have a long history of social and religious change as people have arrived from all over the world, bringing their religious faiths with them. Nowhere is this clearer than in the East End of London, where successive waves of French Protestants, Central European Jews, and Bangladeshi Muslims have settled in the Spitalfields area. One building, now the Brick Lane Jamme Masjid (also known as the Brick Lane Mosque), has adapted to these changes over a period of more than 270 years.

In 1685, the French king, Louis XIV, revoked the Edict of Nantes, which had allowed Protestants limited freedom of worship, and ordered Protestant churches to be destroyed. As a result, many French Protestants, known as Huguenots, left their home country and a large number moved to London. These refugees settled in the East End and established a silk-weaving industry. The community flourished, building their own churches, one of which was the Neuve Eglise in Brick Lane, constructed in 1743 probably to designs by London surveyor Thomas Stibbs. It was a plain brick building in a restrained classical style without a steeple, looking rather like a nonconformist chapel. Inside were rows of pews facing a central pulpit and a gallery provided further seating upstairs.

At the beginning of the 19th century, many of the descendants of the immigrants were moving out into London's suburbs. As the demography of the area changed, the Neuve Eglise became successively an evangelical church, a Methodist chapel, and, with the arrival of many Jews in Spitalfields, a synagogue. The synagogue remained central to Jewish life in Spitalfields until the middle of the 20th century,

However, many of the East End Jews, like the French Protestants before them, moved out to the suburbs and in 1970 the synagogue moved to Golders Green. At the same time, more and more Muslims, mainly from Bangladesh, moved into the Spitalfields area and found work in the textile trade. In the mid-1970s, the former synagogue building changed hands yet again, and was converted to a mosque. The gallery was modified to provide more upstairs space, ablution facilities were added, and the main space was adapted to create a prayer hall, with a mihrab providing a place for the imam to stand and indicating the direction of Mecca.

Classrooms built by the Jewish community in the roof space are used as classrooms for Muslim children and the former vestry house contains the office, kitchen and other facilities. The Brick Lane Jamme Masjid opened in 1976. It can hold up to 3,000 people and was known as the London Great Mosque in its early days. The mosque also has close links with the Bangladesh Welfare Association, which offers advice on housing, welfare, education, IT and other issues.

The architecture of the Neuve Eglise survives to give a hint of the building's history. However, the mosque now has a minaret, designed by DGA Architects as part of a larger scheme of upgrades. Not all mosques have minarets, but this one acts as an effective sign of the building's purpose. The minaret's steel cladding is pierced, and lit from behind in changing colours. This coming together of old and new architecture, reflecting the different faiths that have used the building, is also reflected in the work of the mosque, which fosters interfaith understanding with study circles, tours and conferences. In both its history and its current work, the Brick Lane Mosque exemplifies the diversity of London, and the way its culture and society have been enriched by a pattern of immigration, adaptation and change.

Lady's Well

HOLYSTONE, NORTHUMBERLAND

Sacred wells, associated with a particular Christian saint or event, have a long tradition, linking the faith to specific places, to the life-giving power of water, and to the use of water in the sacred rite of baptism. There are sacred wells in the Holy Land, and there is a holy well in Egypt associated with the desert father St Antony. There have also been a number of holy wells in England. Some of them have disappeared but are recalled in documents or place names; some still survive. Their importance goes back to the early centuries of Christianity in Britain, although wells were also revered in pre-Christian times, when people marvelled at the apparently magical appearance of water out of the ground – such water was sometimes said to have healing powers.

The Lady's Well at Holystone in the Northumberland National Park is one of the survivors. It fills a pool, surrounded by a grove of trees just north of the small, stone-built village, in a beautiful, quiet setting. It was near the Roman road from the fort at Bremenium near Rochester to the coast; this route, after the Romans left Britain, was used by Christian missionaries spreading the faith in northern England.

The well has been associated with three saints, two of whom were important figures in early British Christianity. At first, it was known as St Ninian's Well, linking it to Ninian, who preached the Christian faith in lowland Scotland and northern Northumbria in the early 5th century; he is known as the Apostle to the Southern Picts, and may have come to Holystone on one of his southern missionary journeys. The well is more closely linked to St Paulinus, a Roman missionary who became the first bishop of York and who died in 644. He converted and baptised many people in northern England, including the Northumbrian king Edwin, and Hild, later known as St Hilda, abbess of Whitby. According to legend, Paulinus baptised 3,000 people at Holystone.

In the early 12th century, Holystone became home to a small priory of Augustinian canonesses. Their church was dedicated to the Virgin Mary and as they looked after the well it soon became associated with the saint too. From then on it was known as the Lady's Well. The priory was never large – there were usually only six or eight canonesses resident at any one time – but the well was important to them not only for its past holy associations but also because it provided them with a supply of clean water.

The priory was dissolved, like the country's other monasteries, by Henry VIII in the 16th century, when its value was only £11 per year. Few traces of the priory buildings remain above ground, although a recent dig has uncovered what are probably parts of the foundations. However, the well continued to be used as a source of water, as it is today. The site, which has been enhanced by a cross from Alnwick, is now cared for by the National Trust. It is valued both as a reminder of how important holy wells were to the early church and as an indicator of how a tradition that is no longer part of orthodox Christian observance still speaks to people today.

St Andrew's Church

GREENSTED-JUXTA-ONGAR, ESSEX

Many of England's parish churches are places where Christian worship has taken place for hundreds of years. St Andrew's church, Greensted is one of the most exceptional of these, not just because it has been used for almost 1,000 years, but also because it is largely made of wood. Its wooden nave has proved difficult to date, but Greensted is certainly Britain's oldest wooden church, and is sometimes called the oldest wooden church in the world.

Christian worship probably began at Greensted soon after St Cedd brought the faith to East Anglia in the 7th century. This is the likely date of two previous wooden structures, evidence for which was found during an excavation of the chancel at Greensted in 1960. There seems to have been a church here in 1013, the year in which the remains of Saint Edmund, king and martyr, were moved from London to a new shrine made for them at Bury St Edmunds abbey. The body and its attendants were said to have made an overnight stop at Greensted on their way to the new shrine.

The wooden church that survives today may have been begun some years after that event. Dating the timbers has not been straightforward. Initial dendrochronological work in 1960 put their date at 845. However, more recent research suggests a date sometime after 1053. Even so, the timber nave's survival for so long is remarkable, as is its structure, which is made up of oak logs split down the middle vertically and then set upright in a wooden sill.

Only the nave of the church retains this ancient wooden construction. The church's tower, a timber structure with walls covered in boards and a spire clad in shingles, is much more recent. It may date to the 17th or 18th centuries. The chancel, built of brick, is 16th century, although its lower part, built of flint rubble, may be the remains of an earlier chancel. By the 19th century, the ancient logs of the nave had rotted at their lower ends, so when T H Wyatt restored the building in 1842–9, he removed the oak uprights, built a low brick plinth and replaced the logs in a new sill. Wyatt also rebuilt the roof, although his roof was replaced during a further restoration in 1892.

In this way, the picturesque church at Greensted, with its combination of styles and materials – wooden logs, wooden boards, flint, brick and shingle – evolved over nearly 1,000 years. Although its oak-log structure is unique, the church is typical in its gradual evolution of thousands of medieval and later churches in England. They are testimony not to the church's capacity for producing grandiose architecture but to the efforts of many generations of parishioners to maintain and enhance buildings that were central to their lives. Churches were the places not only where people worshipped every week, but where they were baptised, married and ushered into the next world. Church buildings in turn preserve valuable and fascinating evidence of cultural as well as religious traditions, reflecting changes in building techniques and artistic styles. Few churches have done this for longer than St Andrew's, Greensted.

Guru Nanak Gurdwara

SMETHWICK, BIRMINGHAM

Large-scale Sikh migration to Britain began in the 1950s. This was the period after the Partition of India, when the once-prosperous province of the Punjab, home to the Sikhs, became a troubled frontier zone on the border of India and Pakistan. This disruption, together with a shortage of work at home (and a demand for unskilled labour in Britain) encouraged many people to make the journey. Of those who came, a large number settled in Birmingham. Today, Sikhs are as likely to be doctors, lawyers or businessmen as unskilled workers and while maintaining a strong community, Sikhs have also integrated well into British society.

The oldest Sikh place of worship in England is London's Central Gurdwara (Khlasa Jatha) in Shepherd's Bush, but the largest is the Guru Nanak Gurdwara in Birmingham. Its history began in 1961, when the Sikh community bought and converted a former Congregational chapel in High Street, Smethwick. Before that, the area's Sikhs had worshipped in a school building in Brasshouse Lane, but this arrangement only lasted three years before the congregation outgrew it. This building was outgrown in its turn and the Gurdwara has been rebuilt in a series of operations from 1985 onwards. The first rebuilding phase in 1985 was followed by another starting in 1993 and a third beginning in 1999. The building now has no fewer than eight halls, together with the largest Sikh library in the country. The total congregation is in the region of 10,000, and the building also attracts many non-Sikh visitors.

It is now a striking, white-clad structure, topped with onion domes and finials, flying the Sikh flag, and standing out above its neighbours on Smethwick's High Street. The architecture proclaims the building's Sikh origins, and many gurdwaras have such distinguishing features. However, they are not necessary for a Sikh place of worship. Two key features are essential for such a building: a main hall, where the sacred book of Sikhism, the Guru Granth Sahib, is placed on an elevated throne, and a room for taking communal meals.

The latest addition to the building is a 40,000 sq ft annexe containing a kitchen, a dining hall seating 500, a still larger banqueting hall, classrooms, meeting rooms, and a library. The variety of facilities in the new building reflects the Sikh emphasis on hospitality and community. The free kitchen, or langar, offers free, generally vegetarian, food to all visitors, whether or not they are Sikhs and irrespective of their race, gender, age or social status. This practice is said to have been begun by Guru Nanak, the founder of Sikhism, in the 15th century, and has been central to the faith ever since.

Smethwick's Guru Nanak Gurdwara, with its large building and impressive architectural decoration, is testimony to the size and prominence of the local Sikh population, and to the importance which their place of worship holds for them. More than this, it is a symbol of a community that has become a key part of Birmingham's – and Britain's – society.

Jewish Cemetery

PONSHARDEN, FALMOUTH, CORNWALL

The Jews have a long history in England. They have always been a relatively small section of the population and have had to endure setbacks and persecution, including expulsion in 1290 and restrictions on their activity and right to worship in various periods. By the 18th century, however, the situation had improved. Oliver Cromwell admitted Jews back to England in 1656, and the later Stuart rulers protected them, although they still lacked legal rights. By the Georgian period, the Jewish community was expanding, with some families moving away from major centres of the Jewish population such as London and setting up home elsewhere. The small Jewish cemetery at Falmouth provides moving evidence of these developments and is a rare survival.

The story of the graveyard begins in 1740, when Alexander Moses settled in the town, where he worked as a silversmith. Moses, later known as 'Zender Falmouth', encouraged other Jewish people to settle in the town and a small Jewish community developed. He petitioned the local landowners, the Basset estate, for land for a Jewish cemetery in 1759, and eventually, in 1780, Sir Francis Basset made over a plot of land on the road to Penryn for two burial grounds – one for the Congregationalists, one for the Jews. It is said, however, that there may be Jewish burials on the site from earlier in the 18th century, although the first documented burial was in the 1780s. Alexander Moses himself was buried there in 1791.

The cemetery contains over 50 burials, all dating between 1780 and 1868 except for one of 1913. They show that the Jewish community was never large – there were 10 or 12 families there by the time Alexander Moses died. The plot is surrounded by a wall, part of which also made up the north and east walls of a small mortuary chapel known as an ohel. The remains of the ohel alone make the cemetery very unusual.

The gravestones are mostly carved on local slate and about 30 have legible inscriptions. The earliest stone is uniquely made of granite. Although its inscription can no longer be deciphered, it is thought to belong to Esther Elias, who died in the 1780s. The early stones have Hebrew inscriptions and dates from the Hebrew calendar, but the later ones include English text alongside the Hebrew, detailing the name of the deceased and giving the year of their death using the secular calendar. The later the stones, the more English is included on them, an indication of a change in culture that is also reflected in the way the design of the stones changed, following similar fashions to non-Jewish gravestones in the area.

The Jewish community in Falmouth seems to have prospered in the early 19th century with members involved in various crafts, shipping and allied businesses. However, from the mid-19th century onwards, land communications improved as the railways spread across the country, and Falmouth, a town that relied on sea trade, was badly affected economically. This was reflected in the size of the area's Jewish population, which declined from 14 Jewish families in 1842 to only three families by 1874. The town's synagogue closed in 1879.

Its relatively short history and good state of preservation makes the Jewish cemetery at Falmouth unique. It marks the beginning, rise and decline of a community, without the addition of ranks of 20th-century graves that exist in other burial grounds. Its graves are still visited by descendants of the Falmouth families, who now live as far afield as Israel, but the site has wider significance for its commemoration of a special community and period in Cornish – and English – history.

Stonehenge and its prehistoric landscape

AMESBURY, WILTSHIRE

Stonehenge is probably the best known prehistoric monument in the world. Its impressive circular arrangement of very large stones, up to 30 tons in weight, standing out on the open landscape of Salisbury Plain, is alone enough to make the place famous. The feat of bringing the stones to the site and erecting them with the most basic tools is remarkable in itself. But what makes the place still more significant is that it sits within a large prehistoric landscape full of ancient monuments that offers unique insights into life in England from 3000 BC onwards.

Stonehenge is a complex monument. It is a prehistoric temple, aligned with the movements of the sun, and was built in stages, mainly between 3000 and 2300 BC. Some time around 3000 BC, a ditch with an inner and outer bank was constructed. Just inside the bank the builders excavated 56 pits, known as Aubrey holes, which may have originally held stones or wooden posts and also contained cremated human remains (as does the ditch). About 500 years later, a number of stones were added inside the circular enclosure. These were the enormous sarsen stones, which probably came from Marlborough Downs about 20 miles away and were arranged in an outer circle and an inner horseshoe. In addition there were numerous smaller stones called bluestones, which come from the Preseli Hills in southwest Wales. Although much smaller than the sarsens, these stones each weigh 2 to 5 tons and transporting them would have been a major task. Later, but still in the prehistoric period, the bluestones were rearranged in an outer circle and inner horseshoe, the configuration that remains today.

When Stonehenge was first built, large parts of southern England were still covered in woodland, but archaeologists believe that the site of Stonehenge and its immediate surroundings were mostly open grassland. It is therefore likely that people at the stone circle could see many of the other prehistoric monuments in the area. Today, a variety of structures are still visible as earthworks, giving a vivid impression of a whole landscape that must have had great importance in ancient religion.

A number of these structures are barrows (burial mounds) – the most notable group are the 14 Neolithic and Bronze Age long barrows at Normanton Down, about 1 mile south of Stonehenge. There are also other henges, now visible as circular earthworks, but lacking the stones or wooden posts that they originally had. Woodhenge, consisting originally of six concentric rings of tall wooden posts within a bank and ditch, is about 1.5 miles northeast of Stonehenge. There were henges at Coneybury and West Amesbury (to the southeast). There are also two henge monuments – one a very large earthwork – at Durrington Walls, which was in addition the site of a settlement. A further type of earthwork in the Stonehenge area is the cursus, a long rectangular enclosure surrounded by a ditch and bank, stretching across the landscape; they were built about 1,000 years before the stones were erected at Stonehenge. It is uncertain whether Stonehenge Cursus (and the nearby Lesser Cursus) were built as processional routes or as barriers separating one area from another.

This array of prehistoric structures, laid out across a large stretch of Salisbury Plain, and not far from other major monuments such as Silbury Hill and Avebury, suggests a place where many prehistoric people came to worship, observe the movement of the sun, hold feasts and bury their dead. Such a concentration of monuments, adding up to an entire ritual landscape of the 4th to the 2nd millennia BC, is unique in Britain and internationally important.

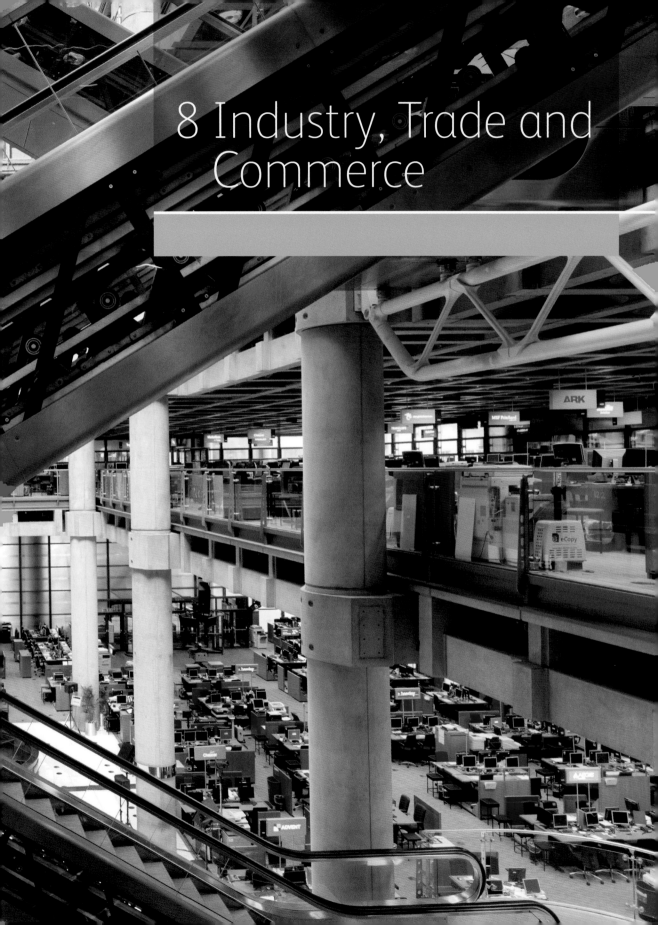

8 Industry, Trade and Commerce

Middleport pottery

BURSLEM, STOKE-ON-TRENT, STAFFORDSHIRE

The pottery industry of Stoke-on-Trent began at least as far back as the 17th century – thriving thanks to the local abundance of potter's clay and fuel for kilns – and by the mid-18th century pots from Stoke were being sold all over the country. By the Victorian period the area was internationally famous for its ceramics and thousands of bottle ovens produced wares that sold all over the world. The industry remains large, but many of the original potteries and their old bottle ovens have been replaced by modern facilities.

Middleport Pottery is a unique survival of the 19th-century industry. It is still a functioning pottery and, although not all of the late-19th-century works survives, it still houses the entire production process, with clay coming in at one end and finished articles coming out at the other.

The origins of Middleport Pottery go back to 1862, when Frederick Rathbone Burgess and William Leigh formed their company Burgess & Leigh and took over an existing business, Central Pottery, in Burslem. They established a brand, Burleigh, based on their two surnames, and moved to Hill Pottery in Burslem before building their own works in 1888 by the side of the Trent and Mersey Canal at Middleport. Unlike many of the existing potteries in the area, which had grown up organically in often cramped and inconvenient locations, this was a purpose-built factory and was built on a spacious site. This gave Burgess and Leigh the scope to lay it out in a way that made production efficient and conditions pleasant for the workers. It was hailed as a 'model pottery'.

When the pottery opened in 1889 it was very impressive, with long ranges of buildings holding the separate departments – the designers' and engravers' department, the printing shop, the hollow-ware pressing shop, and so on, with clusters of bottle ovens in the adjacent courtyards. The factory was sited right next to the canal, making deliveries of clay and dispatches of finished pots straightforward. And the building looked impressive too. It was not only very large but also decorated with terracotta, including an impressive pediment above the entrance with the name Middleport Pottery picked out in ceramic letters.

Like most industrial buildings with a working history of well over a century, Middleport Pottery was adapted over the years. Only one of the bottle ovens now remains and some of the courtyard space is filled with more recent buildings. However, much of the original factory still stands, the single bottle oven is now a rare survivor, and the pottery retains its steam engine. This is a machine from the Boulton factory and was used for mixing clay and providing power for other processes; in addition, steam from its boiler was used for heating and for drying pottery. The engine was used regularly until 1970.

Middleport Pottery was a model Victorian factory, but its success lasted long after the 19th century. Between 1926 and 1931 the renowned designer Charlotte Rhead worked at Middleport. By the time she worked there she was already well known for her lively, colourful floral designs using tube-lining, and her work – modern yet with a wide appeal – was popular. The pottery also produced some very strong designs in the 1950s and 1960s, under designers such as Harold Bennett and David Copeland. However, by 2010 it had fallen on hard times and faced closure because the buildings were in poor condition. Mindful of both the historical importance of the pottery and the loss of jobs if it closed, The Prince's Regeneration Trust stepped in, beginning a £9M project to repair the buildings and revitalise the pottery. The survival of the Middleport pottery as a working factory, embodying well over 100 years of tradition, makes it nationally important.

The Piece Hall

There is no other building in Britain like the Piece Hall. Opened in 1779, this enormous quadrangular structure was designed as a cloth hall, where 'pieces' – 30-yard lengths of cloth woven on hand looms – were sold. It is a unique survivor of a trade that was once vital to the economy of Halifax, Yorkshire, and the whole of England.

The English wool trade had existed since the middle ages and by the 18th century West Yorkshire was the centre of the business. In 1774, the manufacturers of Halifax got together and decided that they needed better accommodation for their regular cloth market. They set up a fund for subscribers and a local businessman and landowner, John Caygill, offered them a parcel of land – a greenfield site south of the city centre – on a 5,000-year lease, on the condition that a cloth hall was built within five years. The manufacturers met the deadline and the Piece Hall opened to the public on New Year's Day 1779.

What the people of Halifax saw at the opening was remarkable: a 66,000 square-foot open piazza surrounded by a three-storey quadrangle. The upper floors of the quadrangle were lined with open arcades and behind these there were 315 rooms, where manufacturers could sell their cloth. The architect of the building is unknown, but whoever designed the Piece Hall produced a structure of great civic grandeur – not just large but noble, with its ranks of Classical columns bringing to mind the splendour of ancient Rome. It was a building of enormous scale and ambition, and a symbol of great local pride. It was also a commercial success. By 1787, 293 of the rooms were in use, 253 of them by cloth-makers from Halifax or nearby, 40 by people from further afield in Yorkshire. In modern terms, about half a million pounds' worth of business was done in the Piece Hall's Saturday morning cloth market. The building had become a major hub of the Yorkshire cloth trade, and was successful for several decades.

By the mid-19th century, however, the textile business was changing. The cottage industry of hand-loom weavers was being replaced by large-scale production in big water- or steam-powered mills, and mill owners were supplying their goods in bulk to buyers. There was much less need for a cloth hall with hundreds of small units and, in 1871 the Piece Hall became a market for game, fish, fruit and vegetables, a role it played for a further century. By the 1970s, with the food market in decline, the building was restored and used for small shops, an art gallery and museum, and other functions. However not all the 1970s repairs were sympathetic to the original building and more work was needed, so recent years have seen a major conservation project, with the Piece Hall's beautiful stonework repaired. Alongside the shops and cafés there is now a major art gallery and a heritage centre that tells the story of the building, Georgian Halifax, and the wool trade that brought the Piece Hall into being. The central courtyard is a welcoming public space with links to nearby cultural facilities.

In northern England many of the mills and factories where cloth was produced still survive to tell the story of how the material was made. But there is only one Piece Hall to represent the trading side of the business. Now conserved and offering valuable commercial and cultural resources to Halifax, it is once more a building that the city can be proud of.

Rochdale Pioneers' Shop

ROCHDALE, GREATER MANCHESTER

The cooperative movement began in the 18th century, but the first successful cooperative society was born in Rochdale in 1844. It was called the Rochdale Society of Equitable Pioneers and its main purpose was to buy and sell goods on a fair-trade basis and to distribute the profits among the society's members. The society was born out of the widespread poverty of the early 19th century, when the coming of large mills with power looms put many weavers out of work and reduced the wages and working hours of those who could find employment; slum housing and high food prices made things still worse.

Rochdale's pioneers were inspired in part by the work of the manufacturer, socialist and cooperative enthusiast Robert Owen, whose textile mill and town at New Lanark in Scotland were well known; Owen was also an advocate of education and trade unionism. The pioneers also drew on their knowledge of earlier cooperative societies. These were mostly not very successful. Many failed because their members had no business experience, or because they could not recruit enough members, or because their finances were scuppered when they offered credit. The Rochdale Pioneers aimed to avoid these pitfalls. They financed the venture by issuing shares at £1 each and securing a loan from the Weavers Association. Finding premises could be difficult for cooperatives, because they faced resistance from conventional shopkeepers who resented the competition they posed. But the Pioneers were fortunate in that a Dr Dunlop offered them the ground floor of a building in Toad Lane, Rochdale. This modest brick-built shop is now seen as the first true home of the cooperative movement in Britain.

The Rochdale Pioneers were successful for several reasons. Their cooperative model was attractive because they divided the profits between members – the famous coop dividend – and made decisions democratically, with each member having one vote. The dividend had real value for poor people in the Victorian period. Few could put enough money by for clothes or to cover emergencies, and the periodic dividend payments helped with this. The Coop's produce was attractive because it was competitively priced and weighed out accurately. Cooperative food was also pure. Many 19th-century food retailers adulterated their food, making the flour in their bread go further by mixing it with cheaper substances such as alum, or adding lead to sweets, copper sulphate to pickles, or iron sulphate to tea. The Pioneers made it a point of principle that they would not do this.

The time was right for the Rochdale Pioneers, and their venture did well. When their success became clear, others followed, and more cooperative societies were formed, often in conscious imitation of the Rochdale Society. This influence was redoubled in 1857, when George J Holyoake published his history of the Rochdale Pioneers. It was said that there were 332 cooperative societies in operation in 1863, 251 of which had started since the publication of Holyoake's book. What began in Rochdale had turned into a movement.

Successful cooperative societies opened extra branches where there was demand, spreading the movement still more. In 1863 a Cooperative Wholesale Society was formed in Manchester, to supply goods to coops. It became a big business, with its own tea plantations in Ceylon and a butter depot in Denmark. The fields in which coops operated diversified too, with cooperative banks, farms, workshops, and housing schemes. What began in Rochdale led to the large network of coops still trading today.

Cromford Mills

DERBYSHIRE

There are many places that were important in the history of industrialisation in Britain but the one with the best claim to have started the Industrial Revolution is Cromford in Derbyshire. This was the place where Richard Arkwright built the first successful water-powered cotton-spinning mill, helping to transform what had been a cottage industry into a business on an enormous scale.

Richard Arkwright, who began work as a barber and wig-maker, transformed the textile industry by using machinery powered by water. It is not known exactly who designed the machines he used. Arkwright took out a patent on a machine called the water frame, a spinning device that drew out the yarn and twisted it tightly, giving it additional strength. He also developed a carding engine to separate and clean the fibres to prepare them for spinning. However, the designs of these machines were not Arkwright's alone – he relied on the work of inventors such as John Kay and Thomas Highs, who devised an earlier form of spinning frame. Arkwright's importance is that he used these machines successfully in a large factory, powering them with a water wheel and using them to turn out large quantities of cotton thread. A single water frame could spin 96 or even 128 threads at a time – work that had until recently been done one thread at a time by hand.

In 1771, Arkwright opened his first water-powered mill at Cromford, a place with a good water supply and away from built-up areas. This was important because textile machinery had already attracted violent protests from hand-workers who were being put out of work by the new technology. The mill itself was very solidly built, to resist the attacks of potential protestors. Because Cromford was isolated, Arkwright had to build accommodation for his workers – and the houses he put up were more solidly built than many working-class houses in cities. In the early days, cloth weaving was still done by hand, so many of Arkwright's houses had a room for a hand loom on the upper floor; the women and children of the household worked in the factory, while the men carried on their trade of hand-loom weaving.

The mill made a lot of money for Arkwright and his business partners, Samuel Need and Jedediah Strutt, and eventually other buildings were put up on the site, including warehouses, offices, and a canal. The mill itself was extended and a further mill was added in 1775. Although the 1775 mill was destroyed by fire in 1890, the site still boasts an outstanding collection of industrial buildings, with good displays and facilities for visitors. Cromford grew too, although it is still a small community by the River Derwent.

But the real significance of Cromford is in the changes it brought elsewhere. Arkwright himself built outside the town, putting up the impressive Masson Mill at Matlock Bath nearby, for example. He licensed his machinery to other mill owners, so factories based on Cromford began springing up. Arkwright's partner Strutt built mills at Belper, together with better workers' housing – Strutt was less flamboyant and more considerate of his workforce than Arkwright. And the spread of mills went far beyond Derbyshire, across northern England and to Scotland, where David Dale founded the village of New Lanark and built a factory based on Arkwright's model.

In the decades to come it became the norm for goods – not just textiles but all kinds of manufactured articles – to be made in factories using powered machinery. Increasingly, during the 19th century steam power replaced water wheels. This transformation could not have happened without those first steps taken by Richard Arkwright at Cromford.

Morris Garage

One of the most important places in the history of the car industry in Britain is not in one of the country's huge industrial complexes, but in a side street in the centre of Oxford. This is where the engineer William Morris began repairing cars and where he built the prototype of his first four-wheeled vehicle, the Morris Oxford.

William Morris was born in 1877 and started work as apprentice to a cycle retailer and repairer. When his boss would not give him a pay rise, he set up on his own – first in a shed in his parents' garden, later in a shop in Oxford High Street. While at the High Street premises he began to make as well as repair cycles. A keen cyclist himself, he also became interested in motorcycles and by 1901 was beginning to produce his own Morris Motor Cycle.

In 1902, to give his manufacture and repair business more space, he rented an old livery stable off the High Street in Longwall Street. Here he also sold and repaired cars and held agencies for several manufacturers, including Humber, Singer and Standard. Although at this time only the rich could afford a car, Morris was successful enough to sell his cycle business and concentrate on four-wheeled transport. So in 1909 he commissioned architects Tollitt and Lee to build a garage on the street frontage of the Longwall Street site. The resulting structure was no dingy workshop. Tollitt and Lee designed an imposing, neo-Georgian building in red brick, with a central pediment, white cornice, and stone entrance archway. Wealthy car buyers were no doubt impressed, and the minds of anyone who was disturbed by the thought of an industrial building popping up among Oxford's ancient colleges would have been put at rest.

Morris moved into the new garage in 1910 and only two years later he was putting together the prototype of his own car, the first Morris Oxford. This was the car that became known as the Bullnose Morris because of its rounded radiator. It was the vehicle that transformed car manufacture in Britain. Because Morris did not have the capacity to produce all the parts of the vehicle himself, he sourced most of them from other makers, putting the pieces together in Oxford. Even so, to produce the cars in sufficient capacity to meet demand, he needed much more space, and by 1914 had moved his manufacturing to Cowley, then outside Oxford. However, he kept the Longwall Street garage for offices.

In his new factory, Morris could make full use of the mass-production methods used by Henry Ford and others in the USA, putting together the cars on an assembly line. He could produce more vehicles more quickly than other British manufacturers and by the 1920s he was making cars not in ones and twos, but in thousands. With the resulting economies of speed and scale, cars could come down in price, and motoring became more and more accessible. Morris's later model, the Cowley Flatnose, both competitively priced and reliable, sold even better than the Bullnose. The motor industry had been transformed, and Morris's work at the Longwall Street garage was the key to this transformation.

Although the old Morris Garage building has been much modified, with a block of students' rooms built behind, the Longwall Street façade has been kept. It is a vivid reminder of the early career of an ambitious and ingenious man who built one of Britain's best known companies, helped to change the way people travelled, and transformed industrial methods by his use of mass production.

Dunston Staiths

During the 19th century the northeast was one of the most prosperous industrial regions of England and what drove that prosperity was coal. Coal from the area was not only used locally but exported in huge quantities to the south on board colliers, but these large cargo ships could not travel far upstream. Horse-drawn wagonways and later steam-hauled railways carried coal from the mines to the navigable rivers; from here it was loaded on to vessels called keels, which carried their precious cargo to the coast, where it was loaded on to the colliers. However, in the late 19th century a way was found of speeding up coal transport by cutting out the keels. Railways were built from colliery to coast, where structures called staiths (or staithes) were built. These were enormous wooden landing stages from which the coal could be transferred from the railway directly to the colliers. The largest staiths were those at Dunston.

The structure built at Dunston is enormous. 1,709 feet long, 40 feet high and 5 feet wide, it was built from over 3,000 tons of North American pitch pine and cost over £120,000 to construct in 1890–93. At its peak it carried over 5 million tons of coal per year. It is said to be Europe's largest timber structure. Its network of timber uprights, horizontals, and braces is as impressive as that of the largest coastal pier – but is totally functional, without any of the decorative flourishes of the seaside. The staiths were working buildings, pure and simple.

The height of the staiths meant that the railway wagons on top were at the correct level to load their cargo into the waiting colliers anchored alongside. The train driver shunted the wagons until they were lined up with a series of hoppers in the floor of the structure; then men called teemers opened trapdoors in the bottoms of the wagons, letting the coal fall into the hoppers and down on to chutes, which directed the coal into the hold of the ship. This was skilled work. The driver of the locomotive had to get the wagons in exactly the right place – and since his engine was behind the trucks, he was working 'blind'. The teemers often had to jump into the chutes to release coal that got jammed, risking being swept down the chutes themselves; and the men who controlled the chutes had to make sure that cargo was level in the hold, to keep the vessel stable.

The huge capacity of the structure, which was the largest of several such landing stages in the area, hugely benefitted the pit owners and the masters of the colliers, boosting the coal trade with the south, at the expense of the keelmen, whose work was all but eliminated. Dunston Staiths carried on working until 1977, by which time coal mining in the northeast was in decline, and were finally completely closed in 1980. In the following decades the structure went through difficult times. It was seriously damaged by fire twice, in November 2003 and July 2010. However, the vast structure was by this time a listed building and a scheduled ancient monument and by the time of the second fire there were already plans for restoration. Following an award of money from the Heritage Lottery Fund, restoration of the staiths has begun and the future of this unique part of the industrial history of the northeast of England is assured.

Old Furnace

In the early-18th century there was a change in the way iron was produced that transformed British industry. The development was a more efficient way of smelting ore to extract iron, and the person who introduced it was Abraham Darby, iron master of Coalbrookdale, in the Severn Valley in Shropshire. The old furnace at Coalbrookdale is the place where Darby turned his ideas into action.

In the 17th century, the usual way of smelting iron was with a blast furnace, fuelled with charcoal and ignited when a blast of air was introduced by enormous bellows. One of the problems with early blast furnaces was the supply of charcoal – producing it was labour intensive, it used up valuable trees that were also needed for other purposes such as ship-building, and too heavy a load of iron ore would crush the charcoal, which restricted the capacity of the furnace.

Ironworking at Coalbrookdale goes back a long way, probably to the Middle Ages – a 'Caldebroke smithy' was recorded at the time of the dissolution of the monasteries. The Old Furnace itself goes back to the mid-17th century and was operating in 1703, when it blew up. Up to this point it would have been fuelled with charcoal. In 1709 Abraham Darby took over the furnace and the adjacent forges. He rebuilt the furnace and began to use a new fuel, coke. Coke was cheaper than charcoal, and allowed larger, heavier batches of ore to be smelted, and this enabled Darby to produce iron goods – mainly cast-iron pots, pans, kettles and the like – more cheaply than his competitors. Darby was not the first to make iron in this way, but his was the first charcoal-fired furnace to work successfully over a sustained period.

The Coalbrookdale business passed from Darby to his son and then to his grandson – both were also called Abraham – and by the time the latter was in charge, the demand for iron was increasing rapidly and the furnace had to be enlarged. The enlarged furnace survives now as a ruin. It bears two painted dates – 1638 (although earlier images show that this was once 1658), which may be the date when the structure was first built, and 'Abraham Darby 1777', which marks the furnace's rebuilding by Abraham Darby III. The structure as it now stands is a square tower containing the inner round furnace, which is built of brick. Originally coke and iron ore were tipped into the furnace from the top, air was forced into the side of the furnace, and two products – molten waste or slag and molten iron were extracted separately from ducts on the sides.

The furnace became the heart of a substantial local iron industry (many other buildings connected to this industry survive in Coalbrookdale) and the growth of industry here made a new bridge over the Severn necessary. The Shrewsbury architect Thomas Farnolls Pritchard proposed building it in iron and the world's first iron bridge, at the place now named Ironbridge, was opened in 1781. Its components were produced by Darby, using iron smelted in his furnace.

By this time Darby was also producing boilers for steam engines and cast-iron rails for horse-drawn railways. In the 19th century, iron was in even greater demand, with steam railways, industrial machinery, buildings and even ships containing substantial amounts of iron. The metal was central to the industrial revolution in Britain, and the development that made possible iron production on a large scale happened in the Severn Valley at Coalbrookdale, where the Old Furnace is one of its most remarkable monuments.

Castlefield Canal Basin

MANCHESTER

The Bridgewater Canal is often called Britain's first true canal (in other words the first to be built independently of an original river) and was built by Francis Egerton, 3rd Duke of Bridgewater, to transport coal from his colliery in Worsley to Manchester. Egerton brought in engineer James Brindley to advise on the construction and route of the canal, and Brindley adjusted the route to make it easier in the future to connect to other waterways. The Castlefield Canal Basin was the Manchester terminus of the canal, although the canal was later extended. When it opened on 17 July 1761, large horse-drawn barges, each capable of taking 30 tons of coal, travelled from Worsley to Manchester. The barges' capacity was ten times that of the largest horse-drawn cart, and dramatically reduced the cost of transport, halving the price of coal.

The coal was unloaded at Castlefield Basin. Here, hoists powered by water wheel could lift 5 tons an hour from a barge. The basin became a commercial and industrial hub, with warehouses, a lime kiln, and a brick kiln built on the site. But the effects of the Bridgewater Canal were felt far beyond the Castlefield Basin. The canal's success and the dramatic reduction in the price of Egerton's coal forced competitors to create canals of their own, and soon a 'canal mania' was sweeping Britain, with more areas being linked by canal, and more rivers newly made navigable. Egerton extended his own canal, beginning by taking it southwest to join the Mersey at Runcorn and provide a link with Liverpool. Later he built an extension from Worsley to Leigh, where it connected to the Leeds and Liverpool Canal's Wigan branch. This not only opened up new markets for Egerton but also pointed towards the potential of a complete canal network. By the end of the 18th century, such a network was a reality – canals had spread across England, connecting cities, manufacturing centres and sources of raw materials, making the country's industrial revolution possible.

The character of the buildings by the canal is shown by the earliest surviving warehouse, Merchants' Warehouse. This is a large four-storey building of the 1820s in brown brick with sandstone dressings. Its canal-side front is dominated by two large arches. These originally led into undercover loading docks, allowing barges to travel right into the building for loading and unloading, taking advantage of the canal's constant water level, unaffected by river flow or tide.

The canal network was key to Britain's industry until the 1820–30s. By this time increasing traffic was putting the canals under strain and the opening of further canals, while it increased capacity, also meant competition – the Manchester and Irwell Navigation was a major competitor of the Bridgewater Canal. In addition, the railways were starting to offer an alternative way of carrying freight. With their faster speed, potential for increasing capacity, and access to many destinations, the railways began to take over the canals' business. Although the Bridgewater Canal survived into the 20th century, the area around the basin was run down by the 1980s. In the following decade, however, regeneration made the area well used once more. Alongside the 19th-century buildings, new buildings have been added to the mix, Merchants' Warehouse and the large Middle Warehouse have been restored, and two new footbridges have been added to the range of 19th-century bridges over the canal. The canal and basin are vibrant once more.

Lloyd's Building

LIME STREET, LONDON

The insurance business has been a key part of the City of London for several hundred years. Its best known institution is Lloyd's of London, an insurance market that was founded in *c* 1688 by Edward Lloyd at his coffee house in Tower Street. Lloyd's original business was in marine insurance, but Lloyd's has grown over the years and is now the world's leading market in specialised business insurance. By the 1970s, Lloyd's was in need of a new building, and an architectural competition was held to find a design. The winner was Richard Rogers Partnership, whose principal architect had recently designed the groundbreaking Pompidou Centre in Paris. Like the Pompidou, the new Lloyd's Building bears little resemblance to any of its neighbouring structures, but manages to combine an outstanding 1970s design with respect for the long tradition of Lloyd's.

Rogers designed the Lloyd's Building from the inside out, fulfilling the requirement for large, flexible office spaces by putting most of the services – staircases, lifts, electrical ducting and plumbing – on the outside. This was also Rogers's approach at the Pompidou Centre, where the ducts and services are finished in bright colours. Putting these functions on the outside makes them easier to service without disturbing the activities going on in the offices. It also gives the exterior its unique appearance, with the staircases, lifts, and bathroom units all clearly visible. In contrast to the Pompidou, however, Rogers clad the Lloyd's services in stainless steel, and the combination of their forms and the shining cladding gives the building its high-tech appearance.

The interior of the building is just as distinctive. The offices are arranged around an enormous atrium, which reaches the full height of the building, culminating in a semi-circular roof of glass and steel. The floor of the atrium houses the central area of Lloyd's, the Underwriting Room (often known simply as 'the Room'). The lower floors of surrounding offices are open directly to the Room, forming balconies with a clear view of the activity below. The upper floors are sealed off from the atrium with glazed panels. Rising through the atrium are a set of escalators giving access to the lower floors and adding a dynamic set of diagonals as a contrast to the soaring vertical columns. The mix of steel, concrete and glass makes the interior as high-tech in appearance as the exterior.

But there is another aspect to Lloyd's: a history that already stretched back around 300 years when the building was put up. This is reflected in several aspects of the design. Rogers preserved part of the original façade of the 1928 Lloyd's building on the street frontage of his own. This seems incongruous architecturally, but it is a clear signpost to the institution's long history. So is the Adam Room, originally designed in 1763 by Robert Adam for the 2nd Earl of Shelburne and used by Lloyd's as a committee room. This interior had been part of the institution's building across the road and was taken apart and reinstalled on the 11th floor of the new building.

One further piece of tradition is the most significant and prominent of them all. This is the Lutine Bell, housed in its Classical rostrum in the Underwriting Room. This bell was recovered from a shipwreck and installed at Lloyd's in the mid-19th century. It was traditionally rung to signal news of an overdue ship – the bell was rung once for a vessel's sinking, twice for its return, and was a way of giving everyone in the building the news simultaneously. Although no longer rung in this way, the bell is a powerful symbol of Lloyd's history and the importance of the institution in Britain's trade and commerce. The architectural and historical importance of the Lloyd's building has been signalled in a different way. In 2011 the building was listed at Grade I. It was at the time Britain's youngest listed building.

The Blue Anchor

HELSTON, CORNWALL

With its small frontage, tightly sandwiched between the two adjoining buildings on Coinagehall Street in Helston, the Blue Anchor pub looks modest. Yet it is also striking, with its stone wall, thatched roof, and window frames painted bright blue, and it is very old. The exact age of the building and its early history as a public house are not known for sure because there are few helpful documents. However, there is a strong tradition that the building was a monks' rest house in the 15th century. This is not unlikely. Many monasteries ran hostelries where pilgrims and travelling monks could stay the night. Beer was a very widespread medieval drink and most places offering hospitality served beer because it was often more hygienic than water from the local supply; the beer was usually brewed on the premises. There would have been a need for such a house of rest in Helston to serve pilgrims on the way to St Michael's Mount. When the monasteries were dissolved in the 1530s, the building may have become one of the town's alehouses – places where beer was brewed and sold, the ancestors of modern pubs.

This is the possible history of the Blue Anchor up to the late-18th century, which is when the first documentary records of the pub occur. One John Dennis is named as the Blue Anchor's landlord in 1778 and by 1782 James James had taken over. However, James's tenure was cut short in 1791 when a pair of soldiers attacked him when he refused to serve them after hours; he was hit in the head with a bayonet and died of his wounds. Further members of the James family carried on running the pub into the early 19th century.

Whatever the details of the Blue Anchor's early history, it is very likely that beer was brewed on the premises from the beginning. The monks would certainly have produced their own beer; the early landlords would have done so too – so-called 'common breweries', which supplied numerous pubs in their area, only became widespread towards the end of the 18th century. The Blue Anchor can therefore claim a very long tradition of brewing on the same site. With the rise of common breweries, and then 'tied houses', pubs that brewed beer became increasingly rare. The Blue Anchor, by contrast, kept on brewing through the 20th century and beer is still produced there today. The pub has a strong claim to a 500-year tradition of brewing.

Today, visitors to the Blue Anchor find a distinctive, traditional pub with cosy rooms, stone walls, stone flagged floors, and a range of home-brewed beers. It is a combination that works well for most customers whether they are locals or come from afar. It is also a reminder that industry and trade – producing goods and selling them – were once much more closely connected than they usually are today. However, with its emphasis on in-house beer, the Blue Anchor is not just a bit of history. With the increasing trend towards smaller, local producers and microbreweries, it is also pointing confidently to the future.

9 Art, Architecture and Sculpture

Angel of the North

GATESHEAD

Since it was installed on its site in Gateshead in 1998, Antony Gormley's sculpture *Angel of the North* has become one of the best known works of public art in the world. At 65 feet high and with a wingspan similar in size to that of a Jumbo Jet, the Angel is probably the world's largest public sculpture and its prominent site on the A1 ensures that it is seen by around 90,000 people every day. Its unique ribbed design and outstretched wings seem to welcome travellers as they approach the city, and the Angel has become a powerful symbol of the regeneration of this part of the Northeast.

The story of the Angel began in 1990, when the Art in Public Places Panel of Gateshead Council decided to allocate the site of a former pithead baths for a major piece of sculpture. In January 1994 Antony Gormley was chosen from a shortlist of artists who had been invited to submit proposals. Gormley worked with the prominent engineering firm Ove Arup & Partners to refine the design and work out the details of construction.

The result was a structure of Corten weather-resistant steel, which contains a small amount of copper to give it its distinctive rich colour. Key to holding the figure together are a series of ribs made of 50mm-thick steel, which are visible from the outside, giving the Angel its distinctive ridged surface. The ribbed construction gives the sculpture great strength – essential because the vast wings have to be able to withstand winds of up to 100 mph. A further practical benefit of this structure was that it allowed the sculpture to be fabricated in sections by specialist plate-workers and welders and brought to the site for assembly.

By February 1998 the fabrication process was complete, the 66ft-deep concrete foundation was in place, and the Angel's components craned into position. People quickly grasped that Gormley had created a powerfully symbolic work. In a place where men had once mined coal in dark and dangerous conditions underground was a green hillside bearing a figure that seemed to reach towards the light and the sky, its enormous wings slightly angled in a gesture of embrace. Gormley highlighted three reasons for building an angel: 'Firstly a historic one to remind us that below this site coal miners worked in the dark for two hundred years, secondly to grasp hold of the future, expressing our transition from the industrial to the information age, and lastly to be a focus for our hopes and fears – a sculpture is an evolving thing.'

The symbolic power of *Angel of the North* has certainly affected many of those who pass it or who choose to stop for a more reflective look. The work has attracted much publicity to Gateshead and created a sense of optimism where previously the abandoned pithead baths had suggested an area in decline. More than this, the Angel is part of a much wider programme of public art in Gateshead, with more than 50 major works, many of them underpinning the regeneration of previously derelict or underused areas such as Gateshead Quays. Many of the works are by artists with international reputations, and this concentration of art had led to further major projects, such as the construction of the Sage Gateshead and the conversion of an old flour mill into the Baltic Centre for Contemporary Art.

These are major projects, but are not merely a matter of bringing in famous artists from outside the area to give the place a veneer of sophistication. Local people are closely involved, from the northeastern firms who worked on the fabrication and assembly of the Angel to the thousands of Gateshead people who enjoy the Sage and the Baltic and benefit from an enhanced urban environment. The Angel's effect is not just broad but deep.

Kelmscott Manor

OXFORDSHIRE

Set near the Thames in west Oxfordshire, Kelmscott Manor is everyone's image of the perfect Cotswold manor house – a building with walls and roof built of Cotswold limestone, mullioned windows, big gables, and beautifully integrated with its setting. It was built by a local farmer, Thomas Turner, in 1571 and extended by one of his descendants in the 17th century. But the house is famous because in 1871 it became the home of the designer, writer and socialist William Morris. Morris lived there until he died in 1896, and the house became enormously influential on his work.

Morris, who rented the house jointly with his friend Dante Gabriel Rossetti, loved Kelmscott precisely because of its Cotswold qualities – its vernacular architecture, the careful craftsmanship with which it was built, and the way in which it was perfectly at one with its surroundings, both its garden and the wider setting on the eastern edge of the Cotswold district. Morris produced many of his most famous fabric and wallpaper designs while at Kelmscott, and the house was also an inspiration and setting for one of his best known books, the utopian fantasy *News From Nowhere*.

Morris's work, together with the way he furnished the house, were hugely influential. His outlook on furnishing was expressed in his famous epigram, 'Have nothing in your houses that you do not know to be useful or believe to be beautiful', and his enthusiasm for items that were made by hand. This was the opposite of the usual Victorian view, which prized cluttered houses and embraced mass-produced goods. His designs also took direct inspiration from the nature that he saw around him – he drew real flowers and birds for use in his fabric designs, rather than copying older designs as many of his predecessors had done.

This approach had a freshness and integrity that appealed to many. Morris's work was influential among other designers and was at the heart of the Arts and Crafts Movement, made up of like-minded artists, designers and craft workers, who rejected the use of machinery and advocated a return to hand work and traditional skills. They also admired the kind of country-based life that the Morrises led and some of them actually relocated to the Cotswolds to try to live a similar life. The area became a centre for Arts and Crafts woodworkers, metalworkers, potters, architects and artists, whose work is now highly valued among collectors and museum visitors alike.

The turn to tradition and hand work also influenced people's view of architecture and heritage. Morris was one of the founders of the Society for the Protection of Ancient Buildings, the organisation that helped to transform the way old buildings, from cathedrals to cottages, were maintained and repaired; it is still one of the country's key conservation bodies.

Socialism, craft work, a new view of design, and conservation – William Morris was influential in all these fields, and his experience of Kelmscott, 'the old house by the Thames' as he called it in *News From Nowhere*, affected them all. Morris knew how important the place was to him – even the London printing press he ran was called the Kelmscott Press – and when he died, he was buried in the nearby churchyard, beneath a simple tombstone designed by his friend and co-founder of the SPAB, Philip Webb. Today, the house belongs to the Society of Antiquaries. It is furnished with Morris's fabrics and wallpapers, and with the simple, hand-made furniture that he loved and promoted. It is a moving memorial to a man who, during his lifetime and in the century since he died, has affected so many fields.

St Paul's Cathedral

LONDON

St Paul's Cathedral in its present form has been a much-loved London landmark for over 300 years. It was built, to designs by Sir Christopher Wren, after its predecessor was gutted in the 1666 Great Fire of London, and the building was consecrated in 1697 and completed in 1710. The years between the fire and the new cathedral's completion were difficult ones for the architect. The church rejected his favoured design, a plan based on an equal-armed Greek cross with a large central dome in Wren's preferred Classical style of architecture. Traditionalists among the churchmen were used to medieval Gothic buildings and wanted a more old-fashioned layout with a long nave and shorter chancel. Wren had to come up with a compromise design, which evolved further during construction.

In spite of the difficulties, the result was a triumph. The churchmen got the type of layout they wanted and London got not only a noble and capacious place of worship but also a soaring Classical building with one of the most widely admired domes in the history of architecture. Wren also made sure that the dome was very tall, by raising it on a 'drum' ringed with stone columns, and topping it with a stone gallery and golden cross. This made the cathedral the dominant structure on London's skyline, a visual focus as you looked across the city – and it remained dominant until planning regulations were relaxed and today's cluster of tall office buildings was constructed around it.

Wren needed all his ingenuity to create the great dome for which the cathedral is now famous. The structure he built actually has three domes, inside each other and each with a different purpose. The inner dome, visible from within the building, is a shallow ceiling that is designed to look good when viewed from the cathedral's floor; the outer dome is the large one that is visible from the outside. Between these two is a concealed cone-shaped dome of brick, reinforced with iron chains, that does the work of supporting the heavy stone gallery at the top of the structure.

The architect enhanced the effect of the design with a memorable west front, with a double row of columns and a pair of towers at either corner. Many visitors to London get their first view of the building from Fleet Street, as they approach from the west, and this façade is what they see. Inside, they are treated to views of receding arches in grey and brownish stone, pale vaulted roofs, and the enormous space of the dome opening up in the centre. The atmosphere is one of awesome spaces that are also light and airy.

As London's Anglican cathedral, St Paul's has become a symbol for the capital, and by extension of Britain too. It is the setting for important religious services and the burial place of people who have had pivotal roles in British history. The cathedral's symbolic status was enhanced during World War II, when it took a hit during the Blitz, but sustained only minor damage while many buildings around the cathedral were destroyed. Although it is now surrounded by taller structures, the power of St Paul's to remind us of past events, to act as a national symbol, and to move the mind and spirit, shows no sign of diminishing.

Tate Modern

BANKSIDE, LONDON

Housed in a converted power station south of the River Thames at Bankside, Tate Modern has become one of the most popular and successful art galleries in Britain. Its cavernous turbine hall and floors of smaller galleries house a rich collection of modern and contemporary art, as well as hosting high-profile temporary exhibitions and powerful installations by contemporary artists, many of them filling the turbine hall and attracting thousands of visitors.

The original Tate Gallery (now called Tate Britain) is on the opposite side of the river at Millbank. It was set up by its founder, sugar company owner Henry Tate, to house two collections – one of British art from the Tudors to the present, and one featuring modern and contemporary art. By the late 20th century, these collections had expanded and the building was too small to display the work adequately and accommodate some 2 million visitors a year. The obvious solution was to move the international modern and contemporary art to a new location, and this prospect became a reality in the 1990s when the old Bankside Power Station became available. The building, designed by Sir Giles Gilbert Scott (also architect of Britain's famous red telephone box and of Liverpool's Anglican cathedral) seemed unpromising in some ways – an industrial structure in a run-down area of London. But it was both large and centrally located.

After an international competition, the architectural firm of Herzog & de Meuron was chosen to mastermind the conversion. They faced the challenge of converting what had been an industrial building full of machinery into a public building fit for displaying a variety of works of art and playing host to millions of visitors a year. They stripped out all the machinery, taking the building back to its steel frame and brick cladding. They converted the boiler house, the northern part of the building, into gallery space. Further space was provided by a large glass extension on top of the building. The turbine hall became an enormous public area, where visitors gathered before ascending escalators to the galleries. The turbine hall also become a display space in its own right, with a succession of often arresting installations by artists such as Anish Kapoor and Ai Weiwei. The architects' approach was to alter the interior's character as little as possible, staying true to Scott's sensibility, with much bare brick and steel – and untreated wooden floors. This not only respected the history and appearance of the power station, but also provided a setting in which the art could shine.

The new gallery was popular from the beginning. Nicholas Serota, the director, had predicted visitors figures around 2 to 2.5 million per year. In the first year 5 million people came through the doors. The programme of exhibitions and installations kept visitors returning, and attracted new ones, so Tate Modern continued to thrive. The gallery introduced new audiences to contemporary art and was instrumental in regenerating a down-at-heel bit of London's riverside. By the early 2000s, the time seemed ripe to extend the gallery.

Herzog & de Meuron came back to build the extension. They added the new galleries on the southern part of the switch house, an area of the building that had been retained by energy company EDF as an electricity substation after the power station closed in 1981. The new structure, a distinctive tower with walls that taper from the base, provides more display space, additional space for artists to make and display new work, and scope for the educational activities that are so important for bringing a new, young audience to contemporary art.

Coventry Cathedral

WARWICKSHIRE

On the night of 14 November 1940, Coventry was hit by one of the most devastating air raids of World War II. Some 4,300 houses were destroyed, along with many shops, factories and the medieval cathedral, where the roofs were destroyed, windows shattered, fittings burned, and the walls seriously damaged. Only the 295-foot spire remained intact. After the war it was decided to keep the ruins of the building and to build a new cathedral alongside, so that the two structures would stand as a reminder of the destruction of war and as a symbol of the renewal and new hope that came with peace.

The British architect Sir Basil Spence won the 1950 competition to build the new cathedral, which he set at right angles to the old, joining the two structures so that the ruins act as a visual prelude to the new building. Spence also linked the two buildings visually by using the same material as the medieval masons – pinkish Hollington sandstone.

Although the building has sandstone walls and a traditional church plan with aisled nave, Spence designed his cathedral very much in a modern idiom. The windows have rectangular panes, with no Gothic tracery; the slender nave columns taper towards their base and support a ceiling divided into a network of straight ribs.

But what is most striking about the cathedral is the way its uses works of art – sculpture, stained and engraved glass, tapestry – to enhance the architecture and focus the mind on the sacred. The effect begins outside, with a great bronze sculpture of St Michael by Jacob Epstein, positioned next to the entrance. The congregation enters the nave through a 70ft-high clear glass window engraved by New Zealand artist John Hutton with more than 60 life-size figures of saints and dancing angels. To the right is the baptistery, lit by another vast floor-to-ceiling window, this time glowing with colour, designed by John Piper. Above the altar is Graham Sutherland's tapestry of Christ in Glory.

There are many other works of art in the building, from the bronze eagle by Dame Elizabeth Frink that adorns the lectern to the wall tablets with lettering by Ralph Bayer. The building is so full of art that some have criticised it for being more like a gallery than a cathedral, but each piece was specially commissioned for its position and role in the cathedral, and for the way it enhances not simply the beauty of the place but also the religious experience of its users. Nowhere is this clearer than in the nave windows by Geoffrey Clarke and Keith New. These windows are set in angled recesses, making them invisible to those entering the building. However, when one walks up the nave towards the altar, and turns back toward the entrance, the stained glass of the windows becomes visible, creating a glowing vision of colour, an image of optimism and revelation.

Coventry Cathedral was consecrated in May 1962. Benjamin Britten's *War Requiem*, specially composed for the occasion, was performed a few days afterwards. The *War Requiem*'s images of the destruction and waste of war balanced the hope symbolised by the cathedral's renewal, just as the ruined medieval church and the architecture of Sir Basil Spence complement one another. Such a balance has also been reflected in the cathedral's ministry, with its strong emphasis on reconciliation – between political and military enemies, between social groups, and between churches. The cathedral is one of the most powerful illustrations of the way art and architecture can be not just symbols, but instruments of hope and peace.

Chatsworth

NEAR BAKEWELL, DERBYSHIRE

The English country house of the Dukes of Devonshire, Chatsworth, is set in a 105-acre garden in Derbyshire. It is for many people the most stunning and memorable of all English country houses, both for its late-17th-century architecture and for the remarkable collection of antiques and works of art that successive dukes have built up – and continue to add to.

Chatsworth was an Elizabethan house that had fallen into disrepair by the end of the 17th century, having been occupied by both sides during the Civil War. William Cavendish, 4th Earl and 1st Duke of Devonshire, began to rebuild it in 1686. He started with the south and east fronts, for which he employed the architect William Talman to create new family rooms and a state apartment. The duke next rebuilt the west front, which he probably designed himself in close consultation with his masons; notable rooms in this part of the house were the painted hall and long gallery. He then hired Thomas Archer to design the north front, making the house substantially complete by 1707. Many of the interiors are sumptuously painted by the leading artists of the late 17th century, including Laguerre, Verrio and Thornhill, and some feature outstanding woodcarvings by a local master carver, Samuel Watson.

The house has been altered in various ways since the 1st Duke completed his building campaign. There was a major remodelling in the early 19th century by the 4th Duke and architect Jeffry Wyatville, which included the addition of a large north wing to the house. The gardens were also developed in the 19th century, when Joseph Paxton (who later designed the Crystal Palace) upgraded them. The water features at Chatsworth are some of the most impressive in any English garden, and the 296-ft Emperor Fountain, built by Paxton, was the highest fountain in the world when it was constructed for the 6th Duke in 1843. Having evolved over time, but still preserving much of its late-17th-century character, Chatsworth is thus one of the most memorable country houses in England: the ultimate 'stately home'.

The quality of Chatsworth is not only about the architecture and garden. The Dukes of Devonshire have built up a remarkable art collection. The oil paintings range from portraits by Gainsborough and Sargent to notable works by Rembrandt and Renoir; the family continues to collect, so there are also works by modern and contemporary artists such as Lucian Freud (who painted numerous portraits of the family). There are outstanding drawings by Leonardo, Raphael, Titian, Rubens, Dürer, and many other old masters and the collection also contains many sculptures from Classical and neo-Classical to modern pieces. Visitors to Chatsworth are also likely to see special exhibitions in or around the house – many of these have been held in conjunction with the auction house Sotheby's, of which the 12th Duke is Deputy Chairman, and have included notable sculpture exhibitions in the garden.

Recent years have also seen a continuing programme of restoration at Chatsworth. The exterior stonework of the house has been cleaned and conserved so that the building now glistens in a golden hue as it catches the sun. Major conservation work has been done on many of the contents, such as the tapestries in the State Drawing Room. With the house well cared for and conserved, the collection growing, and the garden tended and enhanced by sculpture, Chatsworth is cherished more and more.

Yorkshire Sculpture Park

BRETTON PARK, NEAR WAKEFIELD, WEST YORKSHIRE

Set in a 500-acre West Yorkshire country estate, Yorkshire Sculpture Park has established itself as one of the best places to see sculpture in the UK. Its exhibitions and semi-permanent displays feature the work of great British artists such as Henry Moore and Barbara Hepworth as well as sculptors from all over the world such as Ai Weiwei and Jaume Plensa.

The setting is the estate of Bretton Hall, a country house built in the 18th century and surrounded by a large landscape garden. In 1948 the then owner sold the house and its landscape garden to the West Riding County Council. The following year the house opened as a college where art, music and drama teachers were trained.

The roots of the park lie in this educational work. Peter Murray was a lecturer at Bretton Hall College. He wanted to show his students how to encourage pupils to engage with art, and decided to open a sculpture exhibition in the grounds. By looking at sculpture outdoors, he argued, children could get close to the work, walk around it, and experience how its appearance altered in changing light at different times of day. The project gave artists the chance to create new work, exploring the possibilities of open-air sculpture. The experiment, begun with a grant of just £1,000, was a success.

In 2007 the college closed, the buildings were sold to Wakefield Council, and the sculpture park took over running the house and the whole estate. The garden features lakes, lodges, follies, a redundant Georgian chapel and glorious views. These views now form a magnificent framework for sculptures – around 80 are on view at any particular time, allowing visitors to walk up to them and around them, and to enjoy them in what for many is a perfect environment.

In addition, starting in the 1990s, the park has added indoor exhibition spaces, including a large underground gallery that was completed in 2006 and provides 600 square metres of exhibition space, and the chapel, which has been converted to a gallery. Works that combine the qualities of sculpture and architecture, such as James Turrell's *Deer Shelter Skyspace,* also form a memorable part of Yorkshire Sculpture Park. This combination of park and indoor spaces has created an unrivalled setting for the display of sculpture. In addition, the park's position in West Yorkshire places it near to the Hepworth Wakefield and the Henry Moore Institute Leeds, both major centres for the appreciation of sculpture.

Hundreds of thousands of people now come to Yorkshire Sculpture Park every year. They are drawn there for various reasons. Some come for the chance to see work by high-profile international sculptors, some for the unrivalled combination of scenery and art, but most appreciate the unique chance the park gives them to experience sculpture close to, in the round, in a less formal, more inspiring setting than an indoor gallery. For artists too, the place offers special opportunities and challenges. Many have created new work specifically for the park, responding to its natural beauty; others relish the chance to see their work in a new and welcoming context. Sculpture has been placed in open spaces and landscape gardens for centuries, but Yorkshire Sculpture Park takes the combination of art and nature to new levels, offering an unrivalled setting and an absorbing, ever-changing variety of works.

Sutton Hoo

SUFFOLK

One of the most amazing archaeological excavations in British history began in the late 1930s, when the Sutton Hoo ship burial was discovered in Suffolk. It yielded a breathtaking array of finds from the early 7th century, which gave a unique insight into a period of history whose people left virtually no written records and whose story was shrouded in legend.

There are about 18 burial mounds in the Anglo-Saxon cemetery at Sutton Hoo. Most of these were robbed in Tudor times, but two of the mounds remained largely untouched, and in 1938 an archaeological campaign began to excavate the site. What is now called Mound 1 proved to be a ship burial, in which a high-ranking man had been interred in his 90-foot wooden ship. When it was excavated in 1939, it was found that the timbers of the vessel had rotted away, but their imprint remained in the surrounding sand. This gave archaeologists new insights into how such ships were built – their clinker construction, iron rivets, and high stem and stern posts.

Although the body of the deceased did not survive in the acidic soil, inside the ship was a very rich collection of grave goods. These items were of the highest quality, and included regalia suggesting that they belonged to a king, probably Kind Raedwald of East Anglia. Among the treasure were a finely decorated bronze helmet featuring a mask-like face; weaponry such as a sword and spears; beautifully worked objects of gold and garnet, such as the gold Great Buckle; a pair of shoulder clasps in gold and garnet; a shield, silver vessels, and much more. These finds are now displayed in the British Museum in London.

The other burial yielding major finds was Mound 17. This contained the remains of a high-ranking young man and his horse. The deceased was buried with weapons and personal objects such as a comb and the horse harness had fine fittings. These finds are displayed in an exhibition hall at Sutton Hoo itself, alongside replicas of many of the items from the ship burial, to give an eloquent picture of the quality of objects buried at the site.

King Raedwald, the probable occupant of Mound 1, stood at a transitional point in British history. Like many Anglo-Saxon rulers, he was famed as a warrior, scoring a major victory over the powerful kingdom of Northumbria. He was also controversial, because he set up an altar to Christ alongside images of the traditional Norse gods worshipped by his people, who believed that their rulers were descended from the god Woden. The Sutton Hoo finds therefore shed fascinating light on a key period in the country's history, demonstrating not just the high quality of workmanship of which they were capable but also their links with other cultures – some of the silver objects may have come from Byzantium or the eastern Mediterranean. Looking at the finds from Sutton Hoo makes the distant past seem real once more.

Minack Theatre

PORTHCURNO, CORNWALL

During the winter of 1931–32 Rowena Cade, helped by her gardener Billy Rawlings, built an open-air theatre on the Cornish coast near her home, Minack House, Porthcurno. The theatre is set next to a rocky outcrop, with tiered seating, and the backdrop is the sea. Although it has evolved over the years, with more substantial seating and better facilities, the Minack Theatre is still true to Rowena Cade's vision, and still provides a uniquely beautiful and atmospheric setting for drama.

The idea for the theatre came in 1929, when a local amateur group put on *A Midsummer Night's Dream* in a field nearby and repeated the performance the following summer. Its success convinced Cade that a permanent theatre would be a good idea, and when the idea was put forward of a production of *The Tempest*, she realised that her seaside garden would make a good setting. So she and Rawlings spent months moving granite boulders to create a terraced area for seating and the stage area, framed by the natural cliffs and the sea.

The Tempest opened in August 1932 and audiences were enchanted by the production and its setting. The play was well reviewed and its good reception encouraged Cade to turn the Minack Theatre into a permanent venue. Productions continued until the beginning of World War II, at which point the theatre was closed because of the threat of invasion and the need to fortify the coast with barbed wire. During the post-war period, Rowena Cade removed the wartime defences, restored the theatre, and eventually reopened it. She continued to develop it, building structures such as changing rooms, extending the seating, and creating the now well-known stage structure with its circular paved area and partial backdrop of arches. A lot of this work, from steps to seats, was done in concrete, much of which Cade mixed and poured herself. She developed a way of pouring the concrete into formwork, then removing the formwork before the mix had set completely hard, so that she could carve designs into the surface. Sitting on a concrete seat engraved with an abstract pattern or inscribed with the name of one of the theatre's productions is part of the unique charm of going to a performance at the Minack.

Rowena Cade died in 1983, by which time a charitable trust had been formed to run the theatre. It continues to put on an extensive programme of performances, from Easter to September each year. The current management has improved the theatre's facilities further, adding a shop, café, improved dressing rooms and up-to-date sound and lighting systems that bring out the outdoor theatre's potential further. Their work gives local people and visitors the chance not only to see work by a range of visiting companies – including some from overseas – but also to experience theatre in a uniquely beautiful setting. Some 80,000 people enjoy this experience every year, and many more come for a daytime visit to look at the theatre and admire the view. The Minack Theatre is a tribute to one woman's vision and commitment, and a place where magical combinations of theatre and setting can inspire audiences from near and far.

Barbara Hepworth Museum and Sculpture Garden

ST IVES, CORNWALL

Barbara Hepworth was one of the best known British sculptors of the 20th century. Although her work has been exhibited all over the world, she became especially associated with one place, St Ives in Cornwall, to which she moved with her husband Ben Nicholson in 1939. The Cornish town became a haven for artists during World War II, and Hepworth was unquestionably stimulated by this artistic community. She was also inspired by the scenery of Cornwall and by monuments such as the prehistoric standing stones that she discovered there. But even more important was the fact that she found there a near-perfect workspace, Trewyn Studios, where she worked for the rest of her life.

Hepworth described finding Trewyn Studios as 'a sort of magic'. Superficially it is an unremarkable stone building dating to the late 19th or early 20th century, with a slate roof, 250 yards or so from the harbour. But for Hepworth it was ideal, giving her not only a studio but also a yard and a garden where she could both create and display her work. To begin with it was purely a place of work but eventually it also became her home and it was her base for a total of 36 years, taking on more and more of her character over time as she completed work after work, and as the adjoining garden developed, grew with the acquisition of further land, and matured.

Two of Hepworth's main work spaces, the plaster studio and the stone carving studio, remain very close to the way the sculptor left them when she died in 1975. They contain tools and tins of paint that she used, personal items such as her work overalls, and finished sculptures. Small blocks of marble stand ready, as if she were about to take up the chisels and get to work once more. Most of the sculptures that remain at St Ives are personal favourites of the artist and many are displayed in the garden, which she created with the help of her close friend the composer Priaulx Rainier and which was a key part of her living space. Hepworth's living room too retains the imprint of the sculptor's presence, with her own furniture and possessions. Both the white-walled interiors and the greenery of the garden provide harmonious settings for the artist's abstract forms. A range of her work from small sculptures to the large *Four-Square (Walk Through)* of 1966 (opposite) are displayed here.

The whole site – studio and garden together – conjures up the living and working life of a great sculptor. Hepworth must have realised that this would be the case, because she intended the studio to be left as it was and opened to the public when she died. Her will asked that visitors should be able to see not only exhibitions of her work but also the spaces in which it was created. Her family respected her wishes and opened the building in 1976 before passing it to the Tate Gallery in 1980. Tate has carefully conserved the building and contents, and thousands of visitors every year – many of whom also go to exhibitions at Tate's main St Ives gallery – enjoy experiencing this great artist's home and workplace, as well as her garden with its sculptures, all set close to the landscape that so inspired her.

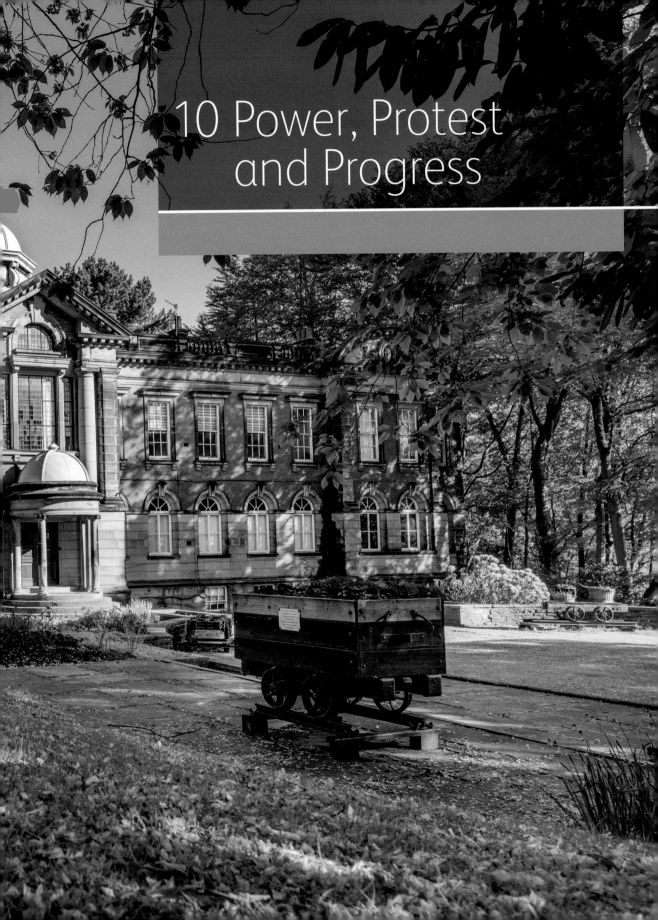

10 Power, Protest and Progress

St Peter's Fields

PETER STREET, MANCHESTER

The tragic event now known as the Peterloo Massacre occurred on 16 August 1819. That day a crowd of some 60,000 people assembled in St Peter's Fields, an area now occupied by part of Peter Street and the Free Trade Hall near the centre of the city. They had come to hear the radical Henry Hunt speak on parliamentary reform. The magistrates, fearing an insurrection, appealed to the military to arrest the people on the platform, and the cavalry charged the peaceful crowd with sabres drawn. Sources vary as to the number of casualties, but around 15 people were killed and as many as 700 were injured.

The massacre summed up the troubles of the times. Since the end of the Napoleonic Wars with the Battle of Waterloo in 1815, the country had suffered widespread poverty and unemployment. Many who did have a job found their wages drastically cut and the first Corn Law banned the importation of foreign corn until the price of British corn reached 80 shillings per quarter. This forced people to buy expensive British grain. It hit city people who could not grow their own food especially hard, but many of them had little chance to appeal to the government about their plight because recently industrialised areas such as Lancashire were very poorly represented in Parliament. Cities such as Birmingham, Leeds and Sheffield had no MP of their own. In Lancashire, Blackburn, Bolton and Manchester were unrepresented except by the county's two MPs. Yet the Greater Manchester area had a population of 409,000 in 1811.

Many Manchester people campaigned for parliamentary reform and found inspiration in radicals such as the orator Henry Hunt and writer William Cobbett. St Peter's Fields became a gathering point for speeches and demonstrations. The military, including poorly trained militias such as the Manchester and Salford Yeomanry, had already appeared at several of these before the events of August 1819. March 1817 saw a large group, mainly textile workers, gather in the square. Some 5,000 of them intended to march to London to petition the Prince Regent about their plight and they arrived with rolled blankets on their backs to use at night. In spite of the fact that their organisers appealed for lawful and orderly behaviour, the calvary were sent in, broke up the gathering, and pursued those who began to march. The so-called 'Blanket March' never achieved its goal.

The crowd that gathered in St Peter's Fields on 16 August 1819 included men, women and children, and they were accompanied by bands. Many carried banners. To the authorities, whose declared intention was to arrest the leaders, mounted soldiers offered the only hope of getting through the crush, so the cavalry was sent in. The horseman hit out with their sabres as they rode through the crowd, targeting those with banners. It was later discovered that the cavalrymen had sharpened their swords before the attack, suggesting that the massacre was deliberate. The uncertainty over the exact number of dead and injured is largely because many people were afraid to admit they were at the demonstration, for fear of putting themselves in further danger.

The tragedy, which became known as the Peterloo Massacre by analogy with Waterloo, did not achieve any immediate reform of Parliament – that had to wait for the Reform Act of 1832. However, it did result in widespread sympathy for the dead and injured protesters, and helped put the reformers on the moral high ground. It inspired a new wave of campaigning, with reformists employing a variety of means, from public speaking to political journalism, satire, and memorial handkerchiefs bearing images of the people in St Peter's Fields. Although the area looks very different today, the massacre that took place there is commemorated with a blue plaque.

Bosworth Battlefield

LEICESTERSHIRE

The Battle of Bosworth in 1485 brought to an end an extended if intermittent period of wars that had lasted 30 years and ushered in the Tudor dynasty, which lasted until 1603. It was thus a turning point in English history, seen by many as the end of the Middle Ages and the beginning of an era in which literature and the arts flourished and England's explorers and navy brought the country much wider influence and power.

The unrest of the 15th century led to the Wars of the Roses, a series of civil wars centred on a dynastic struggle between the houses of Lancaster and York, but involving disputes over other issues, such as the ineffective rule of Henry VI and conflicts between various noble families. In 1461, Edward of York won the Battle of Towton, severely damaging Lancastrian power, and in 1471, as King Edward IV, he won the Battle of Tewkesbury, wiping out the surviving Lancastrians and making his and his heirs' position on the throne seem secure. However, in 1483, Edward IV died and his son, Edward V, ruled only for a couple of months when he and his brother were declared illegitimate by Parliament. Edward IV's younger brother Richard III then became king. With the House of York in disarray as a result of these upheavals, an obscure exile, Henry Tudor, returned and challenged Richard III.

Henry, whose claim to the throne was based on his mother's Lancastrian ancestry, landed at Milford Haven with an army of mercenaries and Lancastrian exiles. As he marched across Wales towards London, he gathered further supporters. He was intercepted south of Market Bosworth in Leicestershire by Richard and a large force. However, in the initial attack, Richard's men proved weak against Henry's forces under the Earl of Oxford, and one battle group failed to come to his aid. Richard then staged a high-stakes attack to try to kill Henry, but this failed and instead Richard was killed. Henry was crowned king immediately, ending Yorkist rule and beginning the Tudor dynasty.

Today the importance of this turning point is acknowledged with a Bosworth Battlefield Heritage Centre at Ambion Hill near Market Bosworth, where the context of the battle and the events of 22 August 1485 are explained to visitors. Ambion Hill was long thought to be the site of the battle – both because of accounts of early historians such as the chronicler Raphael Holinshed, and because of 20th-century research. However, more recent historians have questioned the precise location of the battlefield. Geological work suggests that the area near Ambion Hill was dry land, far from the marshy terrain suggested by earlier accounts. In addition, archaeological research has yielded finds of lead shot in a location some two miles southwest of Ambion Hill. Near here they also unearthed a silver badge depicting a boar. This was the personal emblem of Richard III, and a silver boar would have been worn by a person of high status, perhaps one of the Yorkist king's personal retinue; the find might even indicate the spot where Richard fell. To acknowledge these differences in historical opinion, the boundaries of the designated battlefield area have been extended to include this place, while still embracing Ambion Hill. The continued fascination with the site, the research on its exact location, and the lasting importance of the Tudors, are testimony to the significance of this place.

'Pitman's Parliament'

DURHAM MINERS' HALL, REDHILLS, DURHAM CITY

In the early years of the 20th century, production in the Durham coalfield was reaching its peak. The headquarters of the Durham Miners' Mutual Association, an impressive Gothic building on North Road constructed in the 1870s, was no longer large enough, and the association looked for a site for a new building. They found what they wanted in a plot of land in Redhills. It was owned by St Thomas's Convent, and the nuns had hoped to use it as the site of a new school and college. They commissioned plans from the local architect Henry Thomas Gradon, but could not raise the money to build, so sold the land to the miners. The miners decided to commission Gradon too, impressed by his close knowledge of the problematic sloping site.

Gradon began work on the plans in 1913 and the building was opened in 1915. He produced an imposing building in the Classical style, with central pediment and dome, in a mixture of red brick and stone. The main room is the Council Chamber. It is laid out in a similar way to a nonconformist chapel, with curving rows of seats for delegates, a rear balcony with seating for guests and journalists, and large windows to let in plenty of natural light. The seats are all numbered – there are nearly 200, enough for one delegate from each pit – and they, the wall panelling, and other fittings, are made of good quality Austrian oak. The importance of this room and of the debates held there has earned it the nickname of the 'Pitman's Parliament'. Among the other rooms in the building are richly panelled rooms where miners' representatives could meet with mine owners, offices, and storage facilities for the Association's archives.

The quality of finish inside and outside is impressive, and the whole building – especially the grand marble staircase and the meeting rooms – shows how the miners were keen to create a place where they could meet and negotiate with rich coal owners on as near equal terms as possible. The amount of care put into the design and workmanship also suggests the will to give the miners the best, while also acknowledging their history – the building is adorned by four statues of illustrious miners' leaders made originally for the Association's North Road building. The more recent history of Durham mining is commemorated in various more modern statues in the grounds and a memorial to those who lost their lives in the Easington colliery disaster in 1951.

The building played its part in key moments of Durham's – and Britain's – mining history, from regular pay negotiations between miners and owners, through to the planning of industrial action, culminating in the miners' strike of 1984–5. The place was the scene of both defeats and triumphs, and most of these are recorded in the archives that are stored in the building. The hall is still the local Miners' Association headquarters, although now, with the coalfield no longer mined, the work done there is more concerned with matters such as making compensation claims for those injured during work.

In recent years, the future of the building has been uncertain, but a project to restore it is now underway and the hope is that this place, which embodies so much of mining history in Durham, will be given a new lease of life.

Cable Street
WHITECHAPEL, LONDON

On Sunday 4 October 1936, the British Union of Fascists (BUF), led by Oswald Mosley, had arranged to march along Cable Street, which runs roughly west–east through London's Whitechapel district. The BUF was an extreme right-wing party inspired by the Italian fascists (and adopting a similar black-shirted uniform) and increasingly influenced by the Nazis. It fostered racist views and in particular was vocally antisemitic. To march through an area like London's East End, with its large Jewish population (many of whom had moved to Britain to avoid persecution and pogroms in other countries), was clearly inflammatory. Many of those who objected turned up to oppose the marchers and the police who protected them. The ensuing riot has been known ever since as the Battle of Cable Street.

In the days leading up to the march, the Board of Deputies of British Jews appealed to Jews to stay away, but many, including the recently formed Jewish People's Council against Fascism and Antisemitism (JPC), argued for more active opposition. They petitioned the government to ban the march and when the government refused to do this, a number of groups – both the JPC and socialist organisations – banded together to unite Jewish and non-Jewish objectors to oppose the fascists' inflammatory event.

On the day of the march a huge crowd of anti-fascists (some estimates put the number above 100,000) arrived in the Cable Street area, together with several thousand BUF members and around 6,000 police. The protesters erected barricades across the street to stop the march, piling up ladders, sheets of corrugated iron, even an overturned lorry, to block the street. The police attempted to take the barricades away so that the BUF could proceed.

When the police tried to clear an alternative route for the marchers to avoid the barricades, violence broke out. The protesters countered the use of mounted police with improvised weapons such as chair legs, and locals threw rotten vegetables and the contents of chamber pots on to police from upstairs windows. Adopting the slogan used during World War I and the recently begun Spanish Civil War, they shouted, 'They shall not pass!' Realising he could not control the situation or force a clear way for the marchers, Sir Philip Game, the Commissioner of Police, told the fascists to move away from the area, and Mosley and his followers withdrew westwards beyond Tower Hill.

However, there were soon reprisals, notably the 'Mile End pogrom', during which fascist youths broke Jewish shop windows, looted the shops, and attacked people they believed to be Jewish. In addition, Mosley claimed that he was a victim of the protesters' violence, and there was a rise in recruitment to the BUF in the short term. Over time, though, the event dented the BUF's credibility and the government banned the party in 1940. More positively still, the riot convinced socialists and others that they should tackle more directly the sources of East End poverty that hurt Jew and Gentile alike and encouraged people to join extreme groups like the BUF. So the Battle of Cable Street boosted the Jewish community and has been remembered ever since as a stand against racism and fascism, on behalf of people facing persecution.

A commemorative mural of the struggle, designed by Dave Binnington and painted by him with Paul Butler, Ray Walker and Desmond Rochfort, was created between 1979 and 1983 on the side wall of St George's Town Hall in Cable Street. Using a dramatic distorted perspective, it shows the fighting around a barricade, with protesters hurling missiles, banners waving, and a rearing police horse. This 50-feet high work of art has been occasionally vandalised and restored in turn, and is an arresting and vivid memorial to the stand the protesters made on 4 October 1939.

THE BRISTOL BUS BOYCOTT 1963

EQUALITY

JUSTICE

The Bristol Bus Boycott, inspired by Rosa Parks, the USA civil rights campaigner, was a successful Black-led operation against the Bristol Omnibus Company's ban on Black drivers and conductors. The main players were not the rich or powerful but Paul Stephenson, a Black English youth worker, and Owen Henry, Roy Hackett, Guy Bailey and Prince Brown, Jamaicans looking for a better life in Britain.

In the 1960s Caribbean immigrants had been negotiating with Bristol City Council on problems faced by their community, but their voices went unheard. When a student of Paul Stephenson, Guy Bailey, was refused an interview as a conductor because he was Black, this sparked off the Boycott. Support from Audrey Evans, the African-Caribbean community, Bristol East MP Tony Benn, Bristol University students, fair minded Bristolians, High Commissioners Sir Learie Constantine of Trinidad and Laurence Lindo of Jamaica along with Harold Wilson MP and Julian Gaitskell forced the Bristol Omnibus Company to stop its racist discrimination. This announcement came on 28th August 1963 the day Martin Luther King made his 'I have a dream' speech in Washington D.C. Raghbir Singh was the first person to break the colour bar when the ban was lifted. He was followed by Brennan Samuels and Norris Edwards from Jamaica then Muhammad Rashid and Abbas Ali from Pakistan.

The Bristol Bus Boycott motivated Harold Wilson's government to pass the first Race Relations Act in 1965 and made the campaigners' very British dream a remarkable political coup which was the start of anti-discrimination legislation in Britain.

Bristol University students were joined by fair minded Bristolians in a march supporting the boycott.

This plaque was sponsored by First Bristol, University of Bristol & Bristol City Council, with the support of George Ferguson, Mayor of Bristol.

Raghbir Singh was the first person to be employed as a conductor after the ban was lifted.

THE CAMPAIGN AGAINST RACIAL DISCRIMINATION

Bus Station

BRISTOL

The Bristol bus boycott took place in 1963, after 18-year-old Guy Bailey applied for work with the Bristol Omnibus Company and was told that he could not have a job because he was black. The issue was taken up by a number of leaders of the Caribbean community in Bristol, which led to a boycott, during which black people – and many white people too – refused to travel on the city's bus network. This local stand helped pave the way for national change, and for laws barring racial discrimination in Britain.

In the early 1960s Bristol had a large community of West Indians who had come to Britain from Commonwealth countries to start a new life and fill vacant jobs when the country had virtually full employment. In spite of the fact that they were already British citizens, they faced prejudice and discrimination. It was common, and then quite legal, for landlords to refuse to accommodate people because of their colour or race, or employers to seek only white people when filling vacancies. In addition, racial abuse and violence were not unusual – Guy Bailey recalls being chased by a gang wielding bicycle chains.

When they could find work, people from the Caribbean ended up in mostly poorly paid occupations. In cities other than Bristol, many worked on the buses – London Transport even had a recruitment campaign in Barbados. But in Bristol, this work was not open to black people: the bus company only employed West Indian workers in the garage, away from the public eye, saying that they feared the sight of a black face taking fares would frighten passengers away. The trade union and white workers did little to change the situation, believing that people from the West Indies would accept lower wages and force white people out of work.

Paul Stephenson, a British-born social worker with an African father and a white British mother, remembered the bus boycott of 1955–56 in Montgomery, Alabama, after Rosa Parkes refused to give up her seat to a white man. The Montgomery boycott was a major step in the fight for racial equality in the USA. Stephenson tested the situation by calling the Bristol Omnibus Company and asking if he could send a young man, Guy Bailey, along for a job interview, without mentioning his colour. When Bailey turned up, he was turned away as soon as an employee saw that he had black skin. This sparked Stephenson and a group of other activists, including Guy Bailey and Roy Hackett, to begin a boycott of Bristol's buses. They called press conferences, organised protest marches, picketed bus depots, and staged sit-down protests. Soon the protesters were being joined by white people too. They received support from the leader of the Labour party (and soon to be Prime Minister) Harold Wilson, and from the famous former cricketer Sir Learie Constantine, by then High Commissioner of Trinidad and Tobago.

On 28 August 1963, the day that Martin Luther King made his 'I have a dream' speech, the company announced that their workforce would henceforth be fully integrated. Ragbir Singh, the first non-white employee joined the following month and he was the first of many. The bus boycott led to wider political change. In 1965 the Wilson government passed the first Race Relations Act, banning racial discrimination in public places; the second Act, covering employment and housing, followed in 1968. In 2018 at Bristol Bus Station, a new plaque, showing campaigners Prince Brown, Owen Henry, Paul Stephenson, Guy Bailey and Roy Hackett, together with Ragbir Singh, was unveiled to commemorate this important and influential event.

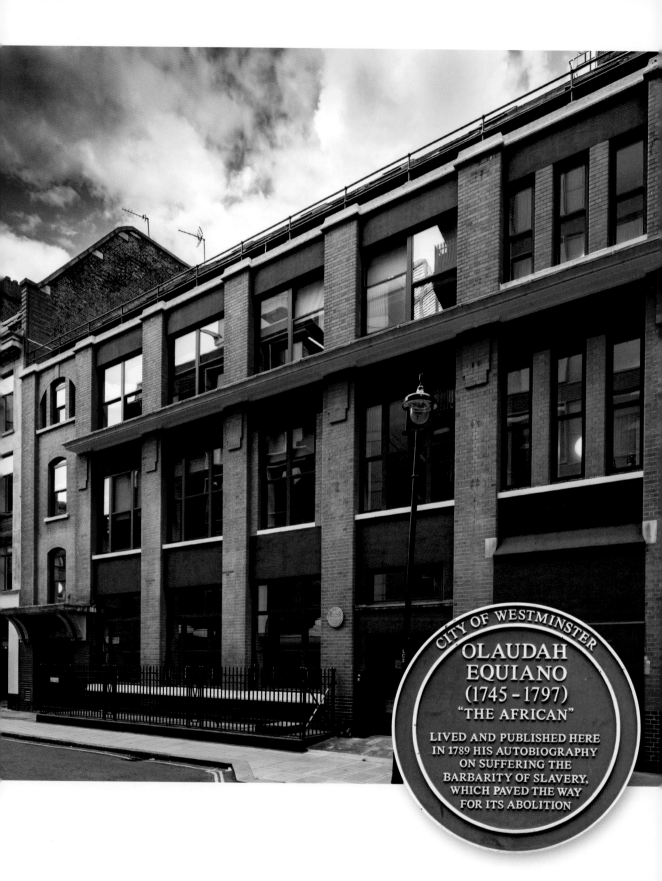

CITY OF WESTMINSTER

OLAUDAH
EQUIANO
(1745 – 1797)
"THE AFRICAN"

LIVED AND PUBLISHED HERE
IN 1789 HIS AUTOBIOGRAPHY
ON SUFFERING THE
BARBARITY OF SLAVERY,
WHICH PAVED THE WAY
FOR ITS ABOLITION

73 Riding House Street

LONDON

On the site of this building in central London (erected in the 1920s as part of the Institute of Biochemistry of the Royal Middlesex Hospital) was the home of Olaudah Equiano (c 1745–97), a pivotal figure in the campaign to abolish slavery. Equiano was a freed slave who published his autobiography, *The Interesting Narrative of the Life of Olaudah Equiano or Gustavus Vassa, the African*, when living in Riding House Street in 1789. The narrative describes his life in some detail, telling how he was born in what is now southern Nigeria, kidnapped by local slave traders, and taken by sea on the middle passage to Barbados and later Virginia. Among his owners were a naval officer Michael Pascal, who named him Gustavus Vassa (after a celebrated Swedish king) and took him to sea, and Robert King, who was a successful merchant and employed him as his valet. While with King, he was able to save enough money to buy his freedom, and he spent several more years at sea.

Equiano had learned to read and write while still enslaved, and he became one of several educated former slaves who made up a group called Sons of Africa, who campaigned for the abolition of slavery by writing to newspapers and MPs and by giving public lectures. Equiano and the other Sons of Africa forged vital links between former slaves and white abolitionists. He was able to tell abolitionist Granville Sharp about the *Zong* massacre, when the captain of a slave ship threw injured and diseased enslaved people overboard so that he could claim on insurance. The work of the Sons of Africa led directly to the 1788 Slave Act, which enforced better conditions aboard the ships that carried enslaved people from Africa to the Caribbean.

When Equiano published his autobiography in 1789 it was immediately popular, going into nine editions. It was one of the first published accounts of a formerly enslaved African's life and is powerfully written, describing the conditions endured by enslaved people on the gruelling Middle Passage across the Atlantic, the degradation of slavery in the Caribbean (and the corruption of the white slave owners), and Equiano's eventual route to freedom and his parallel conversion to Christianity. Prominent white abolitionists immediately seized on Equiano's book as a clear first-hand account of the horrors of slavery. Other enslaved people were writing about their lives, but Equiano's narrative was one of the first, one of the most complete, and probably the best written. Although modern scholars have questioned the veracity of the first part of the book, suspecting that the author may well have been born in Carolina not Africa, the book remains true to the general facts – Equiano clearly spoke to many slaves who had been born in Africa and experienced the Middle Passage themselves.

Equiano died in 1797, but his book lived on, and was translated into many European languages. It became a key text for the abolitionists, much quoted and used as evidence by those who pushed to get better conditions for enslaved Africans and those who campaigned for a total ban on slavery. Its success also encouraged other literate formerly enslaved people to write accounts of their lives, so that the slave narrative soon became a clearly recognisable literary genre, giving those who came after a vivid, authoritative, and often horrific picture of the lives enslaved people had to endure.

Group Operations Room

UXBRIDGE, BOROUGH OF HILLINGDON, LONDON

The Group Operations Room, housed in an underground bunker at what was RAF Uxbridge, on the western outer edge of London, was the control centre for Fighter Command's No. 11 Group, led by Air Vice-Marshall Keith Park, during World War II. It was thus the nerve centre for the part of Fighter Command that protected London and southeast England from the Luftwaffe, and although it was one of four group headquarters, it was the crucial one in the fight to protect the most vulnerable part of Britain from Axis air power. The Group Operations Room at Uxbridge was central to the Battle of Britain and action in occupied Europe was also directed from here, including the fighter activity in such crucial operations as Dunkirk and the D-Day landings.

London and the Southeast underwent merciless bombardment during the Blitz, and aerodromes like RAF Uxbridge were vital targets for the Nazis. The operations room therefore had to be built to be as near bombproof as possible, as well as being able to continue functioning even if the buildings around were put out of action. The room had actually been built in 1938 after the Munich Crisis, to replace an earlier overground headquarters. Bob Creer of the Air Ministry's Directorate of Works and Buildings sited it 60 feet underground. The structure is of reinforced concrete and the walls, floor and ceiling are some 3ft thick. The bunker is entered via steps in a concrete-lined passage and protected by strong steel doors. Inside are rooms dedicated to maintaining a continuous electrical power supply, a secure ventilation system, and reliable telecommunications.

At the heart of the bunker is the operations room itself. This has been preserved as a time capsule, arranged much as it was when Winston Churchill visited it in September 1940. In the middle is the large map table, with its original map, which was used to plot the position of both allied and enemy squadrons. Along one wall is the large board that shows what the various squadrons in Group 11 were doing at that particular point. There are also displays showing the weather conditions at the sector stations where the squadrons were based and clocks indicating the time.

Controllers sat on a raised dais, so that they could see the map table clearly as the plotters – most of whom were women – moved the markers showing the positions of aircraft using information coming in regularly by telephone. Senior RAF and Army officers watched the proceedings from side rooms on a higher level, looking into the room from large glass screens.

The bunker survived the war and was vacated by the RAF in 1958 when No. 11 Group moved to RAF Martlesham Heath. In 1975 it was restored to its appearance in 1940 and in 1985 a museum was opened in the bunker. A major restoration followed in 2015 and there is now a new visitor centre above ground on the site, with displays of replica aircraft, original artefacts, film footage, and oral history material explaining the importance of Uxbridge's secret subterranean bunker.

Martyrs' Tree

TOLPUDDLE, DORSET

The sycamore tree on the village green of Tolpuddle, Dorset, marks one of the meeting places of a group of trade union pioneers who stood up for workers' rights but were sentenced to transportation for their protest. Many people were horrified at the conviction and sentence, and the 'Tolpuddle Martyrs' were pardoned. They became symbols of the movement to secure better pay and rights for workers, and for the risks faced by those trying to campaign for their rights.

In 1799–1800 two Acts of Parliament were passed banning groups of people from 'combining together' to form a trade union or to bargain collectively with their employers. These Acts, known as the 'combination laws', were passed because the government feared that radical opponents would use strikes to bring about political change. However, the Acts were repealed in 1824, partly because of sympathy for workers and partly because they were not effective – workers continued to organise, but did so in secret rather than out in the open.

By the 1820s and 1830s, agricultural wages in England were in decline and in 1833 six men from the village of Tolpuddle in Dorset formed the Friendly Society of Agricultural Labourers to protest about the pay cuts. They had been told by their employer that their wages were to be reduced to 6 shillings per week – the third wage cut in three years. Horrified, they collectively refused to work for less than 10 shillings. They had been meeting under the sycamore tree or in an upper room in a cottage and had sworn an oath of secrecy. But local landowner James Frampton discovered that they had formed a union and sought a way to stop them. What the workers had done seemed perfectly legal, but when Frampton consulted the Home Secretary Lord Melbourne, he suggested an obscure law, the Unlawful Oaths Act of 1797, which prohibited swearing oaths in secrecy. The six men – James Brine, George and James Loveless, Thomas and John Standfield, and James Hammett – were arrested, tried, found guilty, and sentenced to transportation to Australia.

There was a huge protest at the conviction and sentence, with a 250,000-signature petition and a protest march in support of the martyrs. The march was itself a pioneering event and it was successful when in March 1836 the martyrs were pardoned; the six returned to England after various delays between 1837 and 1839. However, they did not find life easy in Tolpuddle, working for landowners who resented their pardon and return, and five of them emigrated to Canada, where they made new lives as farmers in London, Ontario. Several of them wrote about their experiences, and George Loveless's account of the trial and transportation, *The Victims of Whiggery*, was much quoted by later campaigners for workers' rights, particularly the Chartists.

The attempt by the government to defeat the union had failed spectacularly, and the six men of Tolpuddle became national heroes. However, the later progress of trade unions in Britain was far from smooth, with various challenges from employers and governments, and disagreements within and between unions on aims. For all these difficulties, the Tolpuddle martyrs are remembered as courageous and exemplary pioneers. Although historians argue about just how influential they were on the later history of trade unions, the six are now widely commemorated – with an annual festival in Tolpuddle and streets named after the village in places from London to Tasmania.

Physics Laboratory
RUTHERFORD BUILDING, MANCHESTER UNIVERSITY

The New Zealand-born physicist Ernest Rutherford moved to what was then Victoria University, Manchester, in 1907. Educated at Cambridge and the holder of a professorship at Montreal, he was already a leader in his field – his work on the chemistry of radioactive substances and on the disintegration of elements would earn him a Nobel Prize for Chemistry in 1908. He conducted ground-breaking research in nuclear science at Manchester, culminating in an experiment in 1917 which involved the first artificial nuclear reaction. This work heralded the 'nuclear age'.

Rutherford's work between 1914 and 1919 involved experiments in which he bombarded nitrogen gas with alpha particles. He found that the nitrogen nuclei absorbed some of the alpha particles and when this happened, excess energy was produced in the nitrogen nuclei and an oxygen atom and a hydrogen nucleus were emitted. The hydrogen nuclei emitted were actually protons, subatomic particles – Rutherford had discovered a basic building block of the atom. This was a momentous discovery and led to a deeper understanding of atoms and their nuclei, as well as to the development of instruments such as particle accelerators, which could lead in turn to further discoveries and to the creation of a whole new branch of science, nuclear physics.

Rutherford, like most modern scientists, did not work alone. He built up a formidable team at Manchester, working with Hans Geiger (one of the inventors of the Geiger counter), Georg Halevy (who worked with Rutherford and Geiger on the famous 'gold-foil experiment' that helped Rutherford form his theory of the structure of the atom), and James Chadwick (who later discovered the neutron).

What Rutherford did in his Manchester experiments is sometimes referred to as 'splitting the atom'. This is in many ways a misleading term, because Rutherford had not initiated the process of nuclear fission that was later used to generate power. It was, however, a key step in the road to a world transformed by nuclear science – not only in terms of power generation and weapons but also in the way this science has helped to explain the world. Whole areas of physics, from the internal structure of atoms to the way the universe came into being, were opened up by the experiments Rutherford did in Manchester. He continued working in this field, moving to Cambridge to take up the Cavendish professorship, and predicting the existence of the neutron.

The Manchester laboratory was almost new when Rutherford worked there. It had been opened in 1900 and was based on the most up-to-date laboratories in Germany and on recently designed laboratories at Cornell University in New York. By the 1960s the physics department needed to upgrade once more and moved to new accommodation, but the building survived, used first by the psychology department and now by members of the university's administration staff. In commemoration of the influential work of its most famous inhabitant, it is now called the Rutherford Building.

Palace of Westminster

LONDON

The Palace of Westminster has a long history as one of the central places in English history. The original building was constructed as a palace for King Edward the Confessor, and was home to generations of rulers in the Middle Ages. Edward I's 1295 'Model' Parliament, notable for including representatives of the counties and boroughs as well as members of the clergy and nobility, was held there, in Westminster Hall. This vast medieval room (with its stunning timber hammer beam roof of 1393) was generally used for court hearings and grand occasions such as coronation banquets. In subsequent centuries the palace became the regular meeting place of Parliament, although the Houses of Commons and Lords always had to use accommodation that had been designed for some other purpose.

This continued until 1834, when a devastating fire swept through the palace. The entire building was destroyed, with a few exceptions – notably Westminster Hall, the chapel of St Mary Undercroft (formerly the crypt of St Stephen's Chapel), and the 14th-century Jewel Tower. A Royal Commission was appointed to oversee plans for a new building for the Houses of Parliament, and in 1837, a competition was announced for architects for suitable plans 'in the Gothic or Elizabethan style'. The winning entry was designed by Charles Barry.

Barry was a versatile London architect who was highly experienced in Classical and Renaissance work but unsure of his ability in Gothic. He therefore enlisted the help of Augustus Welby Northmore Pugin, who was only in his early twenties but was already an expert in Gothic and one of the greatest advocates of the style. Although historians disagree over which architect should be given the most credit for the building, Barry seems to have been responsible for the overall planning, while Pugin worked on the Gothic details and was mainly responsible for the famous clock tower. The younger man did innumerable drawings for the project, working on everything from window and door mouldings to the design of wallpapers and furniture. Although Pugin was not satisfied with the overall result (believing it to be an essentially Classical building clothed in Gothic ornament), the verdict of history has been positive: the Palace of Westminster is now world famous.

As the home of Britain's Parliament, the palace has seen debates on every issue of substance, from the enfranchisement of women to the country's involvement in war. Since debates, and equally important committee sessions, are now televised, the building's interior is much more familiar to the public than it was and is almost as well known as the celebrated and much photographed Thames-side exterior.

An early Victorian building, the Palace of Westminster is sometimes criticised as being unfit for modern democracy, especially as the number of MPs and peers is now far greater than when Barry produced his plans. These issues have in part been addressed by the provision of new accommodation such as Portcullis House, across the road in Bridge Street. There are still issues, such as the size of the debating chambers, which are packed tightly when everyone attends, but MPs are unwilling to replace the building with a more modern one. The existing building is prized for its heritage of debate and lawmaking, as a piece of Gothic revival architecture, and as a symbol of London and of British democracy. It superb skyline, celebrated clock tower, resounding bell, and ornate interior are not just widely admired, but are also unique.

Index

Picture credits

152   Stonehenge and its prehistoric landscape, Amesbury, Wiltshire. © Historic England Archive, photographer James O Davies (DP157740)

154   Lloyd's building, Lime Street, London. © Historic England Archive, photographer James O Davies (DP161903)

156   Middleport pottery, Burslem, Stoke-on-Trent, Staffordshire. © Historic England Archive, photographer Steve Cole (DP157658)

158   Piece Hall, Halifax, West Yorkshire. © Paul White

160   Rochdale Pioneers shop, Rochdale, Greater Manchester. © Andy Hirst, courtesy of the Co-operative Heritage Trust

162   Cromford Mills, Derbyshire. © Historic England Archive, photographer Alun Bull (DP169103)

164   Morris Garage, Longwall Street, Oxford. © Historic England Archive, photographer James O Davies (DP059532)

166   Dunston Staiths, Gateshead, Tyne and Wear. © Historic England Archive, photographer James O Davies (DP059978)

168 (t)   Old Furnace, Coalbrookdale, Shropshire. Photographer Stewart Writtle

168 (b)   Old Furnace, Coalbrookdale, Shropshire. Photographer Daniel Bosworth

170   Castlefield Canal Basin, Manchester. © Historic England Archive, photographer Derek Kendall (DP074172)

172   Lloyd's Building, Lime Street, London. © Historic England Archive, photographer James O Davies (DP161893)

174   Blue Anchor Pub, Helston, Cornwall. © Historic England Archive, photographer James O Davies (DP220398)

176   Coventry Cathedral, Warwickshire. © Historic England Archive, photographer James O Davies (DP082344)

178   *Angel of the North*, Gateshead. © Historic England Archive, photographer Keith Buck (DP034462)

180   Kelmscott Manor, Oxfordshire © Society of Antiquaries of London/Kelmscott Manor

182–183   St Paul's Cathedral, London. © Historic England Archive, photographer James O Davies (DP159974, DP148446)

184   Tate Modern, Bankside, London. © Tate, London 2018

186   Coventry Cathedral, Warwickshire. © Historic England Archive, photographer Steven Baker (DP164703)

188   Chatsworth, near Bakewell, Derbyshire. © Historic England Archive, photographer Dave MacLeod (28037/13)

190   Yorkshire Sculpture Park, Bretton Park, near Wakefield, West Yorkshire. Peter Randall-Page, *Shape in the Clouds III*, 2014. Courtesy the artist and Yorkshire Sculpture Park. Photo © Jonty Wilde

192   Reconstruction of the Anglo Saxon helmet found at Sutton Hoo, Suffolk. © National Trust Images (CMS/1433773)

194   Minack Theatre, Porthcurno, Cornwall. © Alex Ramsay/Alamy Stock Photo (C951FR)

196   Barbara Hepworth Museum and Sculpture Garden, St Ives. © Tate, London 2018

198   'Pitmans Parliament', Durham Miners' Hall, Redhills, Durham City. © Durham Miners Association

200   *The Peterloo Massacre* by Richard Carlile (1819). Courtesy of Manchester Libraries and Archives

202   Bosworth Battlefield, Leicestershire. © John Critchley (K940708)

204   'Pitmans Parliament', Durham Miners' Hall, Redhills, Durham City. © Durham Miners Association

206   Cable Street, Whitechapel, London. © Historic England Archive, photographer Jonathan Bailey (K031532)

208   Bus Station, Bristol. © Sophie Rhys-Williams

210   73 Riding House Street, London. © Historic England Archive, photographer Chris Redgrave (DP232516, DP232517)

212   Group Operations Room, Uxbridge, Borough of Hillingdon, London. © Historic England Archive (BB000654)

214   Martyrs' Tree, Tolpuddle, Dorset. © Historic England Archive, photographer James O Davies (DP220651)

216   Physics Laboratory, Rutherford Building, Manchester University. © Manchester Heritage Centre

216   Ernest Rutherford (right) and Hans Geiger. © University of Manchester (JRL023068TR)

218   The Palace of Westminster, London. © Historic England Archive, photographer Derek Kendall (DP133849)

Historic England and Ecclesiastical would like to thank all those people who gave time to nominate the wonderful places that mean so much to them. We would also like to express our thanks to the many organisations and people who have provided images, help and advice, without whom this book would not have been published.